TEXAS BLUEGRASS HISTORY

TEXAS BLUEGRASS HISTORY

★ HISTORY ★

HIGH LONESOME ON THE HIGH PLAINS

JEFF CAMPBELL AND BRAEDEN PAUL

THE
History
PRESS

Published by The History Press
Charleston, SC
www.historypress.com

Front cover: (*Clockwise, starting from the top left*) Wood & Wire. *Photograph courtesy of Tony Kamel.* Slim Richey. *Photograph courtesy of Rick Gardner.* John Hartin. *Photograph courtesy of Brandon L. Magnano.* Bill Monroe and the Bluegrass Boys at Gilley's, Pasadena, Texas. *Photograph courtesy of Rick Gardner.*
Back cover: (*Top*) Danny Barnes. *Photograph courtesy of Danny Barnes.* (*Bottom*) Radio Coffee and Beer, Austin, Texas. *Photograph courtesy of Libby Brennan.*

First published 2021

Manufactured in the United States

ISBN 9781467147231

Library of Congress Control Number: 2021941041

CONTENTS

CONTENTS

A SPECIAL THANKS TO THE PICKIN', SINGIN' PROFESSOR

The authors want to give special thanks to Rod Moag, the pickin' singin' professor. Rod's article in the 2004 *Journal of Texas Music History*, "The History of Early Bluegrass in Texas," is an invaluable research document. We are also grateful for his insight, kind words and for pointing us in the right direction, as we compiled this book.

"An academic career to support his music habit" is the best way to describe Rod Moag's life.[1] That career took him on a long and winding road around the world before arriving in the Lone Star State. Professor Moag was born in 1936 and arrived in Austin in 1988.

Rod entered the New York State School for the Blind right before his fifth birthday, and at the age of eight, he began a three-year program playing piano. He started playing guitar at the age of eleven and then moved on to mandolin and fiddle. He also formed his own bluegrass/country band, the Oldtime Hay Balers. Plus, he played in the school's orchestra and dance band and sang in the choir.

His love of radio shows like the *Wheeling Jamboree*, *Grand Ole Opry* and the *National Barn* influenced not only his musical interest but also his academic future. He enrolled in the broadcasting program at Syracuse University and played in a bluegrass band in his spare time.

His academic studies continued at the University of Wisconsin in Madison, where he earned a PhD in linguistics. While in Madison, he was a member of the band the Bluegrass Hoppers. In 1965, he cut a solo 45-rpm

The Bluegrass Hoppers, five University of Wisconsin students specializing in folk music from the Kentucky hills, shown above, will appear on WHA-TV (Channel 21) tonight at 9. Members of the group, left to right, are Earl Spellman, fiddler, bass singer and music graduate student from New York City; Charles Taylor, bass player and history student from Madison; Donald Gale, banjo player from St. Louis, Mo.; Rod Moag, mandolin player, tenor, and the group's MC from Covington, in the hills of New York, N. Y. Jerry Wicentowski, guitarist and lead singer from Brooklyn, N.Y.

Above: While studying at the University of Wisconsin, Rod (*second from right*) played with the Bluegrass Hoppers. In 1967, they released the album *The Country's Come to Town* through Cuca Records. *From the* Capital Times, *May 11, 1967.*

Left: An advertisement from 1974. Rod Moag, picking and singing professor, playing live at Shay's Cafe in Centralia, Missouri. *From the* New Mexico Ledger, *www. Newspapers.com.*

record, *Rachel Ann/Fool Over You*, in Nashville. It was released in the Madison, Wisconsin market in 1967.

Also in 1967, the Bluegrass Hoppers recorded an album, *The Country's Come to Town*. Rod played mandolin and sang tenor on the record. Rod wrote the title song and one other song, the instrumental "The Bluegrass Hop."

After leaving Madison, Rod's travels took him to India, Missouri, Fiji and Michigan before he arrived in Austin in 1988. There, he became an associate professor of South Asian languages at the University of Texas (UT).

While teaching at UT, Rod won second place in both guitar and mandolin contests at the 1994 Round Rock Bluegrass Festival. The year 1995 was huge musically for Professor Moag; he released his first solo CD, *The Pickin'-Singin' Professor*; won the Jimmy Rodgers Yodeling Contest at the Texas Heritage Music Festival in Kerrville; and started a bluegrass show on KOOP in Austin.

From 2000 to 2006, the Professor released six CDs: *Ah-Haa! Goes Grass, A Bluegrass Tribute to Bob Wills*; *Come and Dine*; *Remember Me: Bill Malone and Rod Moag Play the Music of the Bailes Brothers*; and *Bluegrass from The Heart*.

Professor Moag retired from the University of Texas in 2006. However, the music never stops. He joined the band Geezer Grass, which provides entertainment to nursing homes and assisted living centers in the Greater Austin area. Aside from the professor on mandolin, the band includes Marsha Correira on bass, Art Horan on banjo, Jerry Rabun on guitar and vocals and Jim Shaffer on fiddle.

We tip our Stetsons to Professor Moag for his contributions to bluegrass and Texas music.

ACKNOWLEDGEMENTS

JEFF CAMPBELL would like to thank:

- His good friend Roy Wood for a being a musical mentor.
- His mom, Pat Campbell, for introducing him to a variety of musical genres at a young age.
- The Farmers Branch Historical Park and the Bluegrass Heritage Foundation for flying the bluegrass flag in North Texas.
- Ken Brown for allowing him and Braeden Paul to print his detailed history of the Central Texas Bluegrass Association.
- Rick Gardner for allowing the use of his many bluegrass photographs.
- Alan Munde for his stories and time and for the use of his book written with Joe Carr, *Prairie Nights to Neon Lights*. The book is an invaluable resource to anyone who wants to know more about West Texas music.
- Peter Rowan for a two-hour zoom talk that covered everything from San Antonio taquerias to the Allman Brothers (and some bluegrass).
- All of the talented musicians who gave their time to be interviewed for this book.
- His coauthor, Braeden Paul, for agreeing to take on this project in the midst of a pandemic.
- His wife for her enthusiasm and support.

BRAEDEN PAUL would like to thank:

- His dad, Robby Paul, and his grandpa Bobby Paul for introducing him to bluegrass music at an early age.
- His entire family for their love and support.
- Joe Morrow, Buzz Busby and Karl Shiflett for their mentorship.
- Doyle Lawson and countless other musicians for continually inspiring him.
- The Southwest Bluegrass Club for tirelessly promoting bluegrass within the DFW metroplex.
- Mark Porter, the founder of Bluegrass Society of America.
- All of the individuals who gave interviews, pictures and other resources for this book.
- Jeff Campbell for giving him the opportunity to collaborate with him on this project.

INTRODUCTION

If you ask someone to say the first thing they think of when you say, "Texas music," they'll probably respond with Willie Nelson, George Strait or Waylon Jennings. Some may mention Gruene Hall or any of the other numerous dance halls around the state. Others may mention the king of Western Swing, Bob Wills, and his Texas Playboys.

Blues aficionados would probably sing the praises of Blind Lemon Jefferson, T. Bone Walker and Stevie Ray Vaughan. Classic rock fans would mention ZZ Top, Janis Joplin and Johnny Winter.

Fans of folk music traditions could tell you all about the Lone Star State's long history of fiddle contests, polka, Conjunto, Mariachi and Cajun music. There aren't many people who mention bluegrass. Bluegrass music and Texas are not things that usually come up in the same sentence.

However, Texas has a lengthy and somewhat hidden history of bluegrass music—from the traditional to the progressive. Many of these bluegrass musicians played for the love of the music, not for fame or fortune. This story starts with three bluegrass cowboys, the Mayfield Brothers of West Texas, and leads up to the Grammy nominated band Wood & Wire in this new millennium.

The intent of this book is to shed some light on these musicians who have added to the rich and colorful tapestry of Texas music.

1

HOWDY FORRESTER
WENT DOWN TO TEXAS

The first link between Texas and bluegrass probably arose when a Tennessee fiddler headed west to Tulsa, Oklahoma. Howdy was a third-generation fiddler, born in Vernon, Tennessee, on March 31, 1922.

In 1938, Forrester landed a gig on the *Grand Ole Opry* with Herald Goodman's band the Vagabonds. Forrester followed Goodman when he started a new band, the Tennessee Valley Boys. In 1939, Goodman left Nashville to start the Saddle Mountain Roundup on Tulsa's KVOO.[2] Forrester and fellow fiddler Georgia Slim Rutland joined Goodman on his trip out west. The western sojourn carried Forrester down to Texas, and by the time Pearl Harbor was bombed, he was working on his own.[3]

> *We played a certain style and played right on tune, the style that Georgia Slim and I played, but when we went into Texas and Oklahoma, those fellows actually scared the dickens out of me because they were reaching up into the second position and getting notes I'd never seen before. I looked at Slim, and he looked at me, and we said we better get to work here and do something—and we did. If you're in somebody's backyard, you'd better get a hoe just like he's got.*[4]

Howdy and his wife, accordion player Billie "Sally Ann" Forrester, moved back to Tennessee and joined Bill Monroe's Bluegrass Boys. Bill Monroe was quoted as saying, "Howdy was the first man with me to play double-stops."[5] Other fiddlers heard Forrester on the *Opry*, and he "fast became a highly influential fiddler."[6] Gayel Pitchford said:

Howdy Forrester (*right*) playing fiddle with Byron Berline (*left*) and Chubby Wise (*center*) at the Kerrville (Texas) Bluegrass Festival, September 1974. *Photograph courtesy of Rick Gardner.*

Old-time fiddling was undergoing a transition to meet the demands of the newer type of music, where the vocalist's role was on an equal par with the instrumentalists. Working with Monroe, Howard developed new techniques for playing song melodies. He began to play the melody similarly to the way it was sung, but at the end of each phrase, where a singer would normally breathe, Forrester would add an improvised scale portion or an arpeggio, which would lead to the next major melody note on the tonic of the new chord.[7]

In March 1943, at the height of World War II, Howdy was drafted into the navy. This ended his stint as a bluegrass boy. However, his time with Bill Monroe greatly influenced the bluegrass sound by way of Texas.

2

THE FIRST GENERATION OF TEXAS BLUEGRASS MUSICIANS

All Roads Lead to Bill Monroe and the Bluegrass Boys

I t's not a huge surprise that Bill Monroe and the Bluegrass Boys were the largest influences on the first Texas bluegrass musicians. The Mayfield brothers first heard Bill and Charlie Monroe on the radio and later listened to Bill and the Bluegrass Boys on the *Grand Ole Opry*. Fiddler Tex Logan also heard Bill Monroe on the *Grand Ole Opry*. Tom Uhr and his brother heard a DJ talk about a "magical banjo player" coming to San Antonio. That banjo player was Bluegrass Boy Earl Scruggs.

THE MAYFIELD BROTHERS: BLUEGRASS COWBOYS

The story of Texas bluegrass begins in the 1930s in—of all places—Dimmitt, Texas. Dimmitt was home to the ranching Mayfield family. Dimmitt lies in the Texas Panhandle, triangulated by Lubbock to the southeast, Amarillo to the north and Clovis, New Mexico, to the west.

In contemporary culture, telephones, interstates and the internet connect us in a two-way exchange of information, commerce and ideas. However, in the 1930s and 1940s, the only way to reach every corner of the United States was through radio.

This was where the three Mayfield brothers, Herbert, Smokey and Edd Mayfield, heard Bill and Charlie Monroe.

First Entries For Idalou Old Fiddlers' Contest Announced

HALE CENTER, June 22 (Special)—Already entries are being received for the Old Fiddlers' Contest to be staged here July 4 as a feature of the annual Homecoming Day celebration.

The first to enter was Uncle Cal Brown, 71, a hoedown specialist, formerly an Oklahoman. He has lived in Plainview since his retirement several years ago.

The oldest entry to date is Uncle Coke Fullingim, 75, Petersburg cattleman and a resident of the Plains since 1896. He placed s e c o n d among the fiddlers in a contest at Ralls last year and first there the year before.

Dimmitt Youth Enters

The youngest entry is twentyish Smoky Mayfield, Dimmitt cowboy who has won recognition through amateur radio broadcasts.

First prize will be $50; second, $30, and third, $15. There will be no entry fee. Prospective contestants should communicate w i t h Truman Fields, contest chairman, or Glen Wardlaw or Claude Burnett.

The Homecoming program will also include a free barbecue and picnic, a stump speaking for candidates for office a n d a street dance, featuring square dancing at night.

Many men h e r e already are growing beards for the ocasion, and the women a r e searching through attic trunks for pioneer garb. A record-breaking crowd is expected to be on hand.

PEE WEE COLE TRIO
WITH BILL MYRICK & MAYFIELD BROS.
SLED ALLEN ARENA
MONDAY NIGHT JULY 3

ADMISSION $1.00 Tax Inc. WITH PARENTS CHILDREN UNDER 12 FREE

Big Hillbilly Jamboree
TONIGHT 8 P.M.
At Crockett Junior High School

featuring . . .

★ **BIRCH MONROE**
(Bill Monroe's Brother)

★ **ED MAYFIELD**
Brown Co. Jamboree

★ **LARRY RICHARDSON**
5-String Banjo Picker

(above stars formerly with WSM Grand Old Opry)

★ **BILL MYRICK**
Western Roundup

★ **MAYFIELD BROTHERS**
Smokey and Herb

TICKETS AT DOOR

Admission $1.00 Adults   50c Children

Sponsored by the DeMolay Mothers

Left: A 1952 *Lubbock Morning Avalanche* article mentioning Dimmitt cowboy Smoky Mayfield as the youngest entrant in the July 4th Old Fiddler's Contest. *From the* Lubbock Morning Avalanche, *www.Newspapers.com*.

Right, top: Advertisement for Bill Myrick and the Mayfield Brothers opening for the Pee Wee Cole Trio at Sled Allen Arena. *From the* Lubbock Morning Avalanche, *www.Newspapers.com*.

Right, bottom: The Mayfield Brothers featured at the 1953 Big Hillbilly Jamboree. The Jamboree also featured Bill Monroe's brother, Birch Monroe, and *Grand Ole Opry* banjo picker Larry Richardson. *From the* Odessa American, *www.Newspapers.com*.

Edd Mayfield's elementary school classmate Alvie Ivey of Pep remembers driving the family's Model A Ford up to a house window and hooking the car battery to the radio to catch the broadcast of the Grand Ole Opry. *Despite the great distances involved, West Texans could receive WSM's clear channel signal directly from Nashville, and from time to time, thirty-minute segments of the* Opry *were broadcast on the nearby stations in Amarillo and Lubbock.*[8]

The three Mayfield brothers weren't just fans of the *Grand Ole Opry*, they were part of a musical family. Their father, William Fletcher, played fiddle and their mother, Penelope Ruth, played piano and guitar. All the Mayfield children (a total of six boys and two girls) started out on mandolin because it was small and easy to fret.

In October 1939, the most famous mandolin player of all time, Bill Monroe, successfully auditioned for the *Grand Ole Opry*. Edd Mayfield said, "We heard Bill and Charlie Monroe and, later, the Bluegrass Boys and were really excited over what we heard."[9]

All three brothers served their country during World War II. Edd was in the Pacific theater; Smokey was in the European theater and participated in the Battle of the Bulge; and Herbert was in the air force, also participating in Battle of the Bulge and the Normandy Invasion.

After the war, the three veterans returned to West Texas and their ranching life. For their own entertainment, the brothers continued making music. Edd was on guitar, Herb played the mandolin and Smokey sawed the fiddle. Their goal was to replicate the Bill Monroe sound. The band, at that time, featured Earl Scruggs, Lester Flatt and Chubby Wise.

The three Mayfield brothers formed a band devoted to reproducing the style of Bill Monroe exactly—the mandolin, fiddle, open-stringed guitar rhythm and harmony singing—except that they had no banjo. It is truly ironic that they are acknowledged as being the first Texas bluegrass group while lacking the one thing which most fans and scholars alike identify as an absolute requirement for any bluegrass band, i.e. the five-string banjo.[10]

During his time in the army, Edd befriended Bill Myrick from Monroe, Louisiana. Myrick was spending his postwar days as a driver, singer and promoter for Bill Monroe in Louisiana and other southern states.

Edd and Bill had maintained a friendly correspondence in the postwar years. Edd talked Bill into moving to West Texas and joining the brothers as a guitarist and lead singer. Myrick headed west in March 1950, and the group Bill Myrick and the Mayfield Brothers was born.

Soon, the band had a weekly fifteen-minute segment on Lubbock's *KESL Jamboree*. Later in the year, Myrick promoted a short West Texas tour for Bill Monroe and the Bluegrass Boys. Of course, he inserted Bill Myrick and the Mayfield brothers as the opening band. By this time, the Bluegrass Boys featured Jimmy Martin on vocals and guitar, Red Taylor on fiddle and Rudy Lyle on banjo.

The tour through Lubbock, Amarillo, Big Spring and Plainview was an amazing experience for the brothers. It was the first time they had met Bill Monroe, and they were astounded by the band's instrumental virtuosity. Bill was also impressed and complimentary to Edd and the rest of the band. "We did the old song 'Keep On The Firing Line' on the show, and Monroe came around the show and said that was the best rendition of that song he'd ever heard. That gave us alot of enthusiasm, and that's where we got acquainted with Monroe."[11]

Myrick's concert promoting skills and connections led to Bill Myrick and the Mayfield brothers receiving a guest spot on the *Louisiana Hayride* in 1951. At the time, the Shreveport show rivaled the *Grand Ole Opry* in popularity. The band was such a hit that they were included in a *Shreveport Magazine* article, "The novelty of 'FOUR COWPUNCHERS from Dimmitt, Texas' playing hillbilly music appealed to the management, audience and media."[12]

Due to their talent and the crowd reaction, the band was offered a regular spot on the *Louisiana Hayride* that would start within two weeks. However, the regular appearance would never come to fruition. Returning to their hotel, Edd had received a message to call Bill Monroe.

Monroe, remembering Edd Mayfield's strong rhythm guitar playing and singing voice, offered Edd a tryout for the Bluegrass Boys. This caused quite a quandary for the band. However, Myrick, Smokey and Herbert agreed it was an opportunity Edd could not pass up. Joe Drumwright (Bill Monroe's banjo player at the time) remembers Edd's audition.

I was there when Edd tried out. Bill called me up to the hotel and said, "I have a fellow up here, and I'd like to try him out." So, I walked in, and there that ole boy with that big Texas hat and that big Gibson guitar and a thumb pick. I thought what kind of turkey is this? Until I played about two tunes with him. He was great. You couldn't get him out of time, and he played some of the best backing notes you ever heard in your life. Edd was way ahead of his time. There wasn't anyone even close to him back then. He [had] big ole strong hands and could chord a guitar all day."[13]

THE MAYFIELD BROTHERS will be honored with an award during the spring bluegrass jamboree Saturday at South Plains College in Levelland in the Tom T. Hall Production Studio. Concert time is 7:30 p.m., and admission is free. SPC will pay special tribute to the brothers for their pioneering efforts in performing bluegrass music throughout the West Texas area. The brothers are (from left) Herb of Dimmitt, Smokey of Spearman, and Edd, who had performed for several years with Bill Monroe and the Bluegrass Boys before being stricken with leukemia in 1958. (Photo courtesy of Herb Mayfield.)

Mayfield Brothers to be honored

The Mayfields received a tribute and award from South Plains College for their pioneering efforts in the bluegrass field. *From the* Castro County News, *www. Newspapers.com.*

Edd had always been the most performance-oriented of the three brothers. Alvie Ivey recalled that Edd would bring his guitar to school and entertain his fellow students in the basement boiler room.[14]

Edd would make three stints as one of Bill Monroe's Bluegrass Boys. His first stint started on October 28, 1951, when he took part in nineteen recordings with the band. Within a year, Edd left and was replaced by Jimmy Martin. In 1954, Martin, tired of butting heads with Monroe, left to stake out a solo career. Mayfield rejoined the Bluegrass Boys. However, a few months later, he quit and headed back to Texas. In both instances, Edd left for financial reasons; Monroe's pay was not enough to support a family.

In early 1958, Mayfield made his last tour as a Bluegrass Boy. On July 7, 1958, Edd passed away at the young age of thirty-two. Struck with leukemia, he had continued touring with Bill Monroe before succumbing to his illness in Bluefield, West Virginia. Edd was buried in Castro County Memorial Gardens in Dimmitt.

Bluegrass Boy Peter Rowan talked about Edd Mayfield's guitar playing: "Edd was a big influence on the way I play guitar. Neil Rosenberg had started recording the *Brown County Jamboree* in Bean Blossom, and I was able to listen to those recording and learn from Edd.* I called Herb [Mayfield] and told him how much I appreciated Edd."

---

* The recordings of the *Brown County Jamboree* in Bean Blossom, Indiana, were made from 1954 to 1964 and are available at the University of Indiana. Featured on the recordings are Bill Monroe and various Bluegrass Boys, such as Edd Mayfield, Birch Monroe, Kenny Baker, Jim Maynert, Rodger Smith, Del McCoury and Bill "Brad" Keith.

After Edd's death, Smokey only played at family gatherings, while Herbert continued to play music and attend bluegrass festivals. Herbert spent most of his adult life as a designer, builder and welder of cattle feed lots. Herbert was also active in community service. Herb was part of the Fair Board Association, served may years as the president of the Rodeo Association and was a longtime member of the Panhandle Bluegrass Association. He and his wife, Dorothy, also donated money for scholarships to help students attend the South Plains College Bluegrass program in Levelland, Texas.

Smokey spent fifty-one years as a ranch supervisor on the Turkey Track Ranch. Folks say he was the best cowboy they ever had. Smokey and Herb were honored by the South Plains College of Levelland as being pioneers of bluegrass music in the South Plains. They were presented with plaques, and as a special honor, they received belt buckles, recognizing them as Honorary Bill Monroe Bluegrass Boys.[15]

Herbert E. Mayfield passed away on May 29, 2008, in Amarillo, Texas; he was eighty-seven. His final resting place is located in Hart Cemetery in Castro County, Texas.

Arlie Vincent "Smokey" Mayfield passed away on September 11, 2008; he was eighty-four. He was buried in Hansford Cemetery in Hansford County, Texas.

As for Bill Myrick, when Edd joined Bill Monroe, Myrick tried to put together another group for the Louisiana Hayride. Eventually, he moved back to West Texas, settling in Odessa on the advice of Hank Williams. He was

Smokey Mayfield's final resting place. *Photograph courtesy of Donna Barnes.*

In 2006, the *Hansford County Reporter* published an article that Patuxent Music had collected the early recordings of the Mayfield Brothers (1948–1956) and released the collection on CD. *From the* Hansford County Reporter, *www.Newspapers.com.*

hired to play in Hank Williams's band and drive Hank's Cadillac. However, fate intervened when Hank died on New Year's Eve in 1952. Myrick worked for the Odessa Police Department as a motorcycle policeman and became known as the "the Singing Policeman.

Myrick continued to wear many hats as a promoter, bandleader, truck driver and disk jockey. He was instrumental in jumpstarting the careers of Roy Orbison, Elvis and Patsy Cline. He also spent time on the road, traveling with Bob Wills and the Texas Playboys and other national acts. Finally, he retired as a professional musician and worked for three decades at Big Three Industries.

Upon his retirement from Big Three, Myrick started a National Public Radio show, *Silvergrass and Purple Sage*, and sang in the choir at Odessa's First Baptist Church. Bill Myrick passed away at the age of eighty-four on March 12, 2011. He was buried in Sunset Memorial Gardens in Odessa.

Though he was never a household name, the Mayfield Brothers influenced many West Texas musicians, including their nephew Sonny Curtis, Buddy Holly and Waylon Jennings.

The authors want to thank Alan Munde for his research and interviews in Prairie Nights to Neon Lights *and the article "Edd Mayfield 'The Mystery Man,'" written by Doug Hutchens.*

TEX LOGAN: THE FIDDLING ELECTRICAL ENGINEER

An academically minded person would feel pretty accomplished if they received a bachelor's degree from Texas Tech, a master's degree from the Massachusetts Institute of Technology and a PhD from Columbia University.

An inventor would take gratification in patenting a device to improve everyday life.

A songwriter would feel successful if they wrote a Christmas standard that would be recorded by Bill Monroe, Johnny Cash, Emmylou Harris, Jerry Garcia, Dolly Parton, Buck Owens and many others.

A musician would be proud to say they played with Peter Rowan, Mike Seeger, Bill Monroe and Jerry Garcia.

Dr. Benjamin Franklin "Tex" Logan Jr. spent his life doing all of these things and more—an accomplished life well lived. Tex Logan was born in Coahoma, Texas, on June 6, 1927. His father, Benjamin Franklin "Tex" Logan Sr., was an old-time fiddler originally from Centerville, Alabama.

The senior Logan often jammed with Jonah Nix, the father of Hoyle Nix and the grandfather of Jody Nix. The Nix family was steeped in Western swing. Hoyle and his brother Ben founded the West Texas Cowboys in 1946 and patterned the band after Bob Wills and the Texas Playboys.[16] Jody Nix joined the band in 1960 and eventually inherited the band's leadership. Surrounded by fiddlers, it was almost preordained that the young Logan would take up the fiddle, too. However, the path to fiddling greatness took a few twists and turns.

Logan took fiddle lessons as a child, but soon, he became discouraged when he did not get to learn the breakdowns that his father and the others played. Without the desire and passion to play fiddle, though still loving music, Tex turned to the trumpet, an instrument he played all through his school years. Then, in his last year of high school, Logan had an epiphany.

> *It suddenly hit me one day. I remember it plainly. Going home from school, suddenly I had a feeling in my arm. The big thing is the bow. You've got to have that rhythm in the bow or know what to do with the bow. I could feel it and I went in the bedroom, shut myself in there, got my fiddle out. I hadn't played in a long time, and I kind of played, kept sawing around until I could kind of play "Arkansas Traveler." That's how I got pretty good.*[17]

Even though Logan lived in the epicenter of Western swing and the Texas style of contest fiddling, he became a fan and practitioner of "mountain

When Tex Logan fiddles...

Tex Logan in 1977. *From the* Pantagraph Sun, *www. Newspapers.com.*

fiddling." This was due to the influence of the *Grand Ole Opry* and the used records he bought from a local jukebox salesman. Logan formed a band with his two brothers, Russell (on guitar) and Homer (on mandolin). He also traveled and played with transplanted East Texas fiddler H.M. Hubbard.

For the next few years, Tex Logan's musical pursuits took a backseat to his education at Texas Tech. He left Lubbock in 1946 with a degree in electrical engineering. Upon graduation, Tex was accepted into the Massachusetts Institute of Technology (MIT) as a research assistant. Before leaving for the Northeast, he spent his time playing the fiddle in Hoyle Nix's Western swing band.

His time in Boston was a constant pull between music and academics. This would follow him throughout his life; one foot in music and one foot in engineering.

Dr. David Donoho, a professor of statistics at Stanford University, said that Dr. Logan's two careers were not as incongruous as they seemed. In an interview, Dr. Donoho described Dr. Logan's scientific studies as attempts to break signals into their simplest parts and his music as creating complex sounds out of simple notes. "His day job was analysis," Dr. Donoho said. "His night job was synthesis."[18]

In Boston, Tex found his fiddle fever hard to contain. He started playing square dances with guitarist and fellow college student Dick Best. This led to an appearance on WMEX, a local Boston radio station. Though his classes and research work at MIT started to take a back seat, Tex saw his music career take off. That's because Jerry Howorth and Sky Snow heard Logan on the radio and offered him a spot in their band. Jerry and Sky and the Melody Men was a popular northeastern country music group, and Logan joined in the spring of 1947. Jerry and Sky gave Logan the nickname "Tex" to appeal to their New England audiences.

Becoming a full-time musician meant that Tex gave up his assistantship at MIT, which proved to be a misstep when Jerry and Sky moved the band's home base to Albany, New York, on the suggestion of their manager. The band, however, could not acquire gigs or membership in the local musicians' union and quickly disbanded. So, Tex headed back to Texas to work in the oil fields.

The call and lure of music reached the oil field not long after Tex arrived. Ralph's bandmate with the Melody Men Ralph Jones had relocated to Wheeling, West Virginia. Ralph was playing with Wilma Lee, Stoney Cooper and the Clinch Mountain Clan. The band played on Wheeling's *WWVA Jamboree*, a radio show that rivaled the *Grand Ole Opry* at the time. Ralph invited Tex to try his luck in West Virginia.

Tex joined Red Belcher and the Kentucky Ridge Runners. They played on Red's morning radio show and the *Jamboree*. Tex recorded two songs with the bands Kentucky Is Only a Dream and the Old Gray Goose. Later, Tex fiddled for Hawkshaw Hawkins and Big Slim. However, the guilt of letting down his parents in regard to education weighed heavy on Tex. He returned to MIT in 1949.

From 1949 to 1951, Tex juggled music and academics. He played with the Lane Brothers and recorded with the Clinch Mountain Clan. He finally received his bachelor's degree from MIT in 1951.

Also in 1951, Tex wrote "Christmas Time's a Comin'," which was recorded first by Bill Monroe the same year. The song has also been recorded by Johnny Cash, Emmylou Harris, Raffi, Patty Loveless (*Bluegrass and White Snow: A Mountain Christmas*, 2002), Rhonda Vincent, Beautiful Star, Peter Rowan, the Oak Ridge Boys, the cast of the *The Walton's* television show and many others.

The year 1956 was a big one for Tex, as he received his master's degree in electrical engineering from MIT. That year, he also joined Bell Labs in New Jersey, where he developed advances in digital audio and patented an echo canceller used in satellite communications.

Music remained a big part of Tex's life. In 1959, he was invited by Mike Seeger to play on the renowned album *Mountain Music Bluegrass Style*. Then in 1963, Tex accepted an invitation to play at the legendary Newport Folk Festival.

In 1965, Tex received a PhD from Columbia University for his dissertation, "Properties of High-Pass Signals." Most of the 1960s and the early 1970s, for Tex, was consumed by work, family and playing bluegrass festivals. One of the highlights was playing with the Grateful Dead's Jerry Garcia and the members of Old and In the Way, such as Jerry, Peter Rowan, David Grisman and Vassar Clements.

In 1974, with one of Tex's engineering colleagues, Larry Shepp, Tex developed the Shepp-Logan phantom, what became the standard for computerized tomography image reconstruction simulations of the human head.

It was at the Bean Blossom Festival, where both Tex and Peter Rowan were playing as "floaters," that a new band was born. In 1978, Peter Rowan and Tex Logan formed the Green Grass Gringos. The band performed, toured, cut an album in Europe and recorded songs that were released on albums under Rowan's name. Peter Rowan described a trip with Logan back to his hometown of Big Springs:

> *Tex was playing a Western swing dance with Hoyle Nix's band, and I sat in with my acoustic guitar. No one could really hear me, so feeling left out, I jumped off the bandstand and started dancing with the girls, the wives and daughter of these West Texas ranchers. When I went back up on stage, Tex was mad; "You don't ever leave the stage and dance with the girls!"* [19]

The 1983 album *Revelry*, featuring Peter Rowan on vocals, acoustic guitar and mandola, Tex Logan on fiddle and Greg Douglass on lead and slide guitar. *Author's collection.*

By 1983, Tex realized he could not carry on with the dual careers of music and engineering. So, the Green Grass Gringos said "adios."

Tex formed a local band, the Northeast Seaborn Band. The band kept him involved in music without the travel. He retired from Bell Labs as a research mathematician in 1993.

Benjamin Franklin "Tex" Logan Jr. passed away on April 24, 2015, at the age of eighty-seven, in Morristown, New Jersey. His final resting place is at Spade Cemetery in Mitchell County, Texas. Joseph Bottum said:

> Out in a little mid-Texas town—Coahoma, population nine hundred or so—a smart boy realizes he's good at math and science, and down that road lies an absorbing and successful career. But out in that same mid-Texas town, a quick boy realizes he's also pretty good at playing the fiddle. And the wise man, into whom those boys grow, finds a way to use both his talents in interesting ways: always having a second string to his bow as he passed through life.[20]

The authors want to thank Alan Munde for the research in Prairie Nights to Neon Lights.

Tom Uhr

In the 1930s, a fiddler by the name of Bob Wills founded a group known as the Texas Playboys. Once Wills and his band began releasing recordings, their unique style of music, known as Texas swing, would catch the ears of a number of listeners and aspiring musicians. Among those who found themselves drawn to Wills and his Texas Playboys was the Uhr (pronounced like "ore") family who lived in Olmos Creek near San Antonio, Texas.[21]

The year 1935 was a significant one for Bob Wills as well as the Uhr family. For Wills, it was when he and his Texas Playboys released their first ever recording on Okeh Records. For the Uhrs, it was when they welcomed Albert Thomas, who was referred to as Tom, to the world on November 20.

Tom found himself interested in music at a very early age, in part because of the band his family had formed. This group, led by Uhr's father, was largely influenced by the music of Bob Wills, as many bands had been throughout the 1930s and 1940s. Before Tom could even play an instrument, he began writing his own songs at the age of nine, a gift and passion that would remain with him for the rest of his life and would continually serve him well throughout his musical journey. Once he started playing the guitar,

Tom Uhr in 1983. *Courtesy of Juan del Valle.*

Tom began making local appearances along with his family band, and he began occasionally performing on radio shows.[22]

In 1946, Tom and his brother happened to hear a radio disc jockey excitedly talk about a "magical banjo player named Scruggs, who plays with the Bluegrass Boys!" The group, led by Bill Monroe, was in town, as they were due to give a performance in San Antonio. After hearing this disc jockey declare that everyone had to see this magical banjo player, eleven-year-old Tom, along with his sixteen-year-old brother, made his way to the San Antonio Municipal Auditorium to see Bill Monroe and the Bluegrass Boys. Along with Monroe leading the band on mandolin, the group consisted of Earl Scruggs on banjo, Lester Flatt on guitar, Robert "Chubby" Wise on fiddle and Howard "Cedric" Rainwater on upright bass. This configuration is considered to be the ensemble that defined the bluegrass sound. That night, Tom found himself enthralled with Scruggs's dynamic three-finger picking style.[23] Like many others, he eventually sought out a banjo and began to learn the nuances of this unique approach to the instrument. Once Uhr had learned a few different songs on the banjo, his family band made them a part of their stage shows.

In 1958, Tom began his career as a coach and teacher in Irving Independent School District (ISD). Even as he became more active coaching sports such as Track, Football and Basketball, Uhr still maintained a musical presence by making guest appearances on the *Big D. Jamboree* in Dallas. The music he was performing at this time fell more into what would come to be known as rockabilly. These brief performances on the *Jamboree* caught the attention of the newly formed 20th Century Fox Records (a subsidiary of the 20th Century Fox Film Studios), which signed Uhr to the label as a single vocalist. For the next two years, Tom recorded various selections of original material for 20th Century Fox. The label also made reference to his day job by marketing him as "the Singin' Coach."

The *Big D. Jamboree* was interested in making Tom a member of its regular cast, but he realized that it would cause conflict with his coaching career. He ultimately turned down the offer from the *Jamboree*, but he did not stay away from music altogether. In 1961, Uhr, along with other sports coaches, formed the Coaches Three, a group that capitalized on the folk boom of the era, popularized by groups such as the Kingston Trio, Peter, Paul and Mary, the Weavers and the Brothers Four. Tom performed with the trio until 1965.[24] A year later, in 1966, he formed a group that would ultimately make its mark in Texas bluegrass history.

3

THE SECOND GENERATION

The 1960s would prove to be an important time in bluegrass music. Artists like Flatt and Scruggs, Bill Monroe and the Stanley Brothers were beginning to gain an even greater following, in large part due to the American folk revival.

While all of that was unfolding, Texas-based musicians, such as Joe Bass, Johnnie Martin and the House Brothers, were beginning to organize their own groups. Just one year after the first bluegrass festival was held in Fincastle, Virginia, Irving resident Tom Uhr transitioned from playing commercial-based folk music to form the Shady Grove Ramblers in 1966. Holly Bond soon followed in 1969 by forming the Bluegrass Texans. All of these bands not only released studio recordings but also performed and remained active for several decades. The most notable of these bands were the Shady Grove Ramblers and Joe Bass's Double Mountain Boys, both of which ran consecutively from the 1960s to the 2010s.

THE SHADY GROVE RAMBLERS

In the 1960s, there was a revitalized interest in bluegrass music thanks, in part, to the American folk revival, which occurred in the mid-1960s. Another major factor was the development of bluegrass festivals, the first being held in 1965 in Fincastle, Virginia. When San Antonio native Tom Uhr decided to leave a folk music trio he had been a part of to form his own bluegrass band, the timing could not have been better.

The Shady Grove Ramblers performing at the Irving Masonic Lodge in July 2019. *From left to right*: Kevin Kirkpatrick, Loyd Hinch, Tom Uhr and Chris Burkhalter. *Photograph courtesy of Kirk Green.*

As with Tom's previous group, the Coaches Three, the Shady Grove Ramblers were based out of Irving, Texas. Beginning in 1966, the original configuration consisted of Uhr on guitar and lead vocals, Eddie Green on mandolin and tenor vocals and Bob Emberton on guitar.[25] Eventually, other players joined the group, such as Buddy King on banjo and harmony vocals and Stovey Stovall on upright bass. In 1967, Oklahoma native Loyd Hinch joined the Ramblers, playing fiddle and, occasionally, mandolin. Hinch, who moved to Dallas in the early 1960s as an insurance salesman, met Tom Uhr at a local jam session, and they quickly became friends.[26] After Eddie Green departed the band in the 1970s, Loyd became the mandolinist and tenor singer, a position he held for the next forty-five years. Although many musicians came and went through the Ramblers, Tom Uhr and Loyd Hinch were the two constants that maintained the group's signature sound.

The Ramblers released their first album, *Tree Pickin'*, in 1972. While this project primarily consisted of renditions of material previously recorded by other artists, such as John Denver, Flatt and Scruggs and Charlie Moore, it also featured four songs penned by Tom Uhr. As the Shady Grove Ramblers continued making music together, Uhr's original material became even more of a focal point within the band's studio recordings and live stage shows, something that truly set them apart from the majority of the Texas-based bluegrass acts in existence. One such song that gained notoriety was "You May See Me Walkin'," which was written by Tom in 1953. Years later, the song was heard by a young rising country singer named Ricky Skaggs, who then recorded it in 1981. It quickly became a number-one hit in the country music charts. This resulted in Tom receiving the Horizon Award from American Society of Composers, Authors and Publishers (ASCAP) later that year. The Shady Grove Ramblers eventually recorded their own version of "You May See Me Walkin'," which appeared on their 1983 record, *Remembering.*

Unlike Tom Uhr's previous musical ventures, he found being a bluegrass guitarist and singer much more compatible with his day job as a schoolteacher and athletics coach in the Irving ISD. As the Shady Grove Ramblers gained popularity, they found themselves playing at various events, all on weekends. As bluegrass festivals became more prominent throughout the United States, the Ramblers would often find themselves traveling in their 1950s green-and-white tour bus to different parts of the country, such as Arkansas, Louisiana, Missouri, Colorado and California. In several cases, the band would be on the bill with prominent legends in bluegrass music, such as Bill Monroe, Mac Wiseman, and Jim and Jesse. At one point in their career, the Ramblers were a part of the cast of the *Cowtown Jamboree*, a show that was held at Panther Hall in Fort Worth. The band often found itself opening for legendary names in country music, such as Ernest Tubb, Marty Robbins, Gene Watson and Lynn Anderson among others. In 1983, they performed for the Cotton Bowl Committee to welcome the two competing teams in that year's college bowl game, Pittsburgh and Southern Methodist University.[27]

One such musical legend the Ramblers befriended was fiddle player Chubby Wise. Wise, who previously performed with Monroe, Flatt and Scruggs and country singer Hank Snow, started recording his own studio albums and making stage appearances under his own name in the early 1970s. Like some artists, Wise did not employ a band of his own. In most cases, when he was scheduled to play a festival or another event, he would generally use a locally based group to serve as his backing band during a performance. Whenever Chubby was playing in the Southwest or anywhere else the Shady Grove Ramblers were performing, it was not uncommon for him to call on them to help him out. In September 1989, Wise, along with the Ramblers, performed at Tres Rios Park in Glen Rose, Texas. This particular show was recorded and subsequently released as *Chubby Wise with the Shady Grove Ramblers.* This recording captures Wise's unique style and several of his signature tunes, such as "Orange Blossom Special," "Maiden's Prayer" and "Florida Blues." It also features an original song by Tom Uhr, "Fiddle, Wooden Case and Bow," which was written in Chubby's honor.

As the Shady Grove Ramblers continued to record albums and make public appearances, they received numerous accolades, most notably at the Society for the Preservation of Bluegrass Music in America (SPBGMA) Awards. From 1974 to 1978, they were named "Vocal Band of the Year." In 1974, Tom Uhr was awarded best male vocalist, an honor that he would go on to receive multiple times throughout the Ramblers' career. That same year, Loyd Hinch was awarded mandolin player of the year.[28]

The Ramblers went on to become one of the longest-running bands in Texas bluegrass history. They recorded a total of seventeen albums, all of which were released on the band's own label, Grove Records. Their final project, *That Old Clock*, was released in 2007. Throughout that decade, as well as the 2010s, the band's performance schedule mostly consisted of appearances at festivals and local events within the Southwest region.

On Tuesday, September 1, 2020, Tom Uhr passed away at the age of eighty-four, which marked the end of the nearly fifty-four-year-long career of the Shady Grove Ramblers and the end of an era in Texas bluegrass music history. Longtime sideman Loyd Hinch passed away four months later on January 20.

THE HOUSE BROTHERS

The House Brothers were so powerful and soulful with their music.
It would touch you down deep—especially hearing it in person and
experiencing, up close, the power they had.
—Karl Shiflett[29]

In the small town of Chattanooga, Oklahoma, on September 28, 1936, William House (who would be referred to as Billy) was born. Two years later, in 1938, his younger brother named Jerry was born in Alex, Oklahoma.[30] It wasn't long before they discovered a music that would later come to be known as bluegrass.

Just one year after Jerry's birth, Billy, along with the rest of the Houses, moved to Watsonville, California. One Saturday night in 1941, the family of nine tuned in to WSM's *Grand Ole Opry*, which was being broadcast from the War Memorial Auditorium in downtown Nashville, Tennessee. Just five years old at the time, Billy House recalled being drawn to this mandolin player with a powerful tenor voice. That man's name was Bill Monroe, and he was being backed by his band, the Bluegrass Boys. It's worth noting that, at this particular time frame, the sound of bluegrass music wasn't fully formed yet; however, certain elements of it were definitely present during this particular chapter of Monroe's musical journey. During the first few years of the Bluegrass Boys' existence, Bill Monroe employed a four-piece band consisting of mandolin, fiddle, guitar and upright bass.

In 1945, the House family packed and moved again, this time, to Leon County, Texas. In December of that same year, Bill Monroe took to the stage of the Ryman Auditorium with his latest configuration of the Bluegrass Boys, introducing the audience to the dynamic banjo stylings of a young North Carolinian named Earl Scruggs, as well as the blueprint for what would come to be known as bluegrass music. Billy and Jerry House wouldn't hear these new sounds in person until 1959, when they made a trip to the Municipal Auditorium in Shreveport, Louisiana, to attend a live broadcast of the *Louisiana Hayride*.

The *Louisiana Hayride*, which began in 1948, was similar to the *Grand Ole Opry* in that it was a live country music show that gained a wide following through Saturday night broadcasts. Eventually earning the label "Cradle of the Stars," the *Hayride* became a launching pad for many aspiring artists, most notably Elvis Presley and Hank Williams Sr. In 1958, an alumnus of Bill Monroe's Bluegrass Boys, Jimmy Martin joined the show's cast, bringing his raw, soulful brand of bluegrass to the Municipal Auditorium stage.

Of all the artists Billy and Jerry House saw on the *Louisiana Hayride* in 1959, they were most struck by Jimmy Martin, particularly his young banjo player, J.D. Crowe of Lexington, Kentucky. Crowe, who first saw Earl Scruggs in person at the age of twelve, was taken with his unique approach to the instrument and set out to learn every nuance of Scruggs's style. J.D. Crowe

The House Brothers in 1980. *Courtesy of Billy House.*

went on to be one of the most influential banjoists in bluegrass music history. Billy House cites Martin's performance that evening as the moment he and his brother Jerry decided to become bluegrass musicians themselves.[31]

Shortly after that, the House brothers began making music of their own. Billy took up the guitar, and Jerry began playing the

The House Brothers and the Cannan Valley Boys on stage around the 1960s. *Courtesy of Billy House.*

mandolin-banjo, an instrument which combines the body of a banjo with the neck of a mandolin. The brothers also started singing duets together from their childhood.

In 1962, Billy and Jerry formed their own band, the House Brothers and the Canaan Valley Boys. While their music was strictly gospel, the instrumentation was bluegrass oriented. The original configuration of the Canaan Valley Boys consisted of Billy on guitar, Jerry on mandolin, Carson Day on banjo and Jack Gideon on vocals and tambourine. The group primarily performed in churches during this particular period. Billy House, who was a minister at this time, would often preach during these engagements.

By 1967, the House Brothers and the Canaan Valley Boys had their own live radio show on the Christian network KSKY in Dallas. Two years later, in 1969, the wife of bluegrass musician and promoter Bill Grant was attempting to listen to the *Grand Ole Opry*'s Saturday night broadcast on 650 AM but tuned into 660 AM by mistake. The House Brothers happened to be on the air that evening. Impressed by what she heard, she encouraged her husband to book them for his upcoming bluegrass festival in Hugo, Oklahoma. As a result, the House Brothers were the first Texas-based bluegrass artists to be booked for Bill Grant's inaugural bluegrass festival, which was attended by more than 1,200 people.[32]

Also in 1969, the House Brothers released their first studio album with the California-based record label Rural Rhythm. The label's owner, Jim O'Neal, contacted Jerry House with a proposal to record him, Billy and the Canaan Valley Boys. The self-titled release, *The House Brothers and the Canaan Valley Boys*, was an unconventional recording debut. One of O'Neal's standard practices was requiring an artist to have a total of twenty songs on an album, a departure from the usual ten to twelve selections. As a result, the group recorded shortened versions of many of the songs they typically performed on stage or during their radio broadcasts.[33] Rural Rhythm sold all of their releases by mail order only, which didn't afford the House Brothers much in the way of exposure. Jim O'Neal passed away in 1982, and Rural Rhythm was purchased by Sam Passamano in 1987. In subsequent years, the label released albums by some of the most well-known artists in bluegrass music, such as Russell Moore and IIIrd Tyme Out and the Lonesome River Band.[34]

As Billy, Jerry and their band started appearing at more events outside of churches, they began incorporating secular music into their repertoire. By 1976, they had become a full-fledged bluegrass outfit, which resulted in them dropping the Canaan Valley Boys from their name and marketing themselves solely as the House Brothers. By this time, the brothers had made appearances at various other festivals, such as the Glen Rose Bluegrass Jamboree and Rod Kennedy's Bluegrass Festival in Kerrville. One of the House Brothers' ultimate highlights was performing "I'll Meet You in Church Sunday Morning" on stage with Bill Monroe himself at Hermann Park in Houston, Texas.

Throughout their history, the House Brothers had various band members, among whom were Buddy King, Richard Suddreth, Johnny Thorn, Gary Hutchens and even Billy House's son David. Perhaps the most noteworthy was George Giddens, who performed with the group on fiddle. He would later go on to play fiddle and mandolin with Rodney Dillard, a founding member of the legendary bluegrass band the Dillards.

In 1980, the House Brothers were named the first-place winners of the bluegrass band contest at Bill Grant's festival in Hugo, Oklahoma. Their performance from that year was recorded, and several songs were featured on the album *Live at Hugo*, which was released on Bill Grant's Kiamichi label.

The House Brothers continued to perform and record until 1990, marking the end of a remarkable twenty-eight-year-long career. On May 13, 1995, Jerry House passed away at the age of fifty-six. Billy House continued to remain active as a minister, presenting his gospel music and testimony to churches and prison units around Texas. In 2017, Billy began learning how to construct guitars. This led to him restoring various vintage guitar models, such as Harmony and Silvertone.

SOUTHWEST BLUEGRASS CLUB

As Tom Uhr continued to perform with the Shady Grove Ramblers, he noticed that there were multiple organizations in Oklahoma and Arkansas devoted to promoting the bluegrass music genre. Realizing that there wasn't any association like that in Texas, Uhr, along with his wife, Anne, and several others, began formulating plans to start a nonprofit organization with the idea of "bringing bluegrass friends together," as their mission statement reads.[35]

On October 13, 1974, the first official meeting of the Southwest Bluegrass Club was held at Chisholm Park in Hurst, Texas. The club began with a total of eighty-four charter members. From there, multiple goals were set, such as providing scholarships to young and aspiring bluegrass musicians to further their craft, promote bluegrass concerts featuring local and national touring artists and publishing a monthly newsletter.[36]

Over the course of the next several decades, the Southwest Bluegrass Club met at various locations, such as the visitor's center in Grapevine, the Kirkwood United Methodist Church in Irving and the Just Off Main Coffeehouse in Grapevine. Throughout its history, the club has seen many of its goals come to fruition.

One particular aspect that was most important to the Southwest Bluegrass Club was educating generations, young and old, about what bluegrass music is and how to play it. This was done in several different ways. The Southwest Bluegrass Club provided scholarships to several different aspiring bluegrass musicians, often for them to go to different music camps, such as Camp Bluegrass in Levelland, started by Alan Munde and Joe Carr, and Gerald Jones's Acoustic Music Camp in Arlington. Slow jam sessions also became a regular feature at club meetings, allowing new, aspiring musicians to begin making music with others while playing at a pace they were most comfortable with. Several young musicians who attended SWBC meetings would go on to have professional music careers, among them was Grammy-winning guitarist Brad Davis, as well as sisters Martie Erwin Maguire and Emily Erwin Strayer, the founding members of the Dixie Chicks (now known as the Chicks).

The club also hosted different festivals and concerts over the years. One of their first events was an outdoor festival in Perrin, Texas, which was later hosted by the Mitchell family.[37] They've also hosted concerts featuring several acclaimed bluegrass acts, such as Audie Blaylock and Redline, Blue Highway and Joe Mullins and the Radio Ramblers. Oftentimes at club meetings, locally based groups would give performances, among them Ellis County Bluegrass, Blue Valley and the Shady Grove Ramblers.

Another big goal of the club was met when it began publishing its monthly newsletter. Since its first issue, *Bluegrass Reflections* has contained articles written about various members within the organization, as well as book reviews and other topics related to bluegrass music. The newsletter also featured listings on various bluegrass events around Texas and other regions, such as Oklahoma, Arkansas and Louisiana.

Although the organization has had various presidents, directors and members over its long history, the Southwest Bluegrass Club has been devoted to carrying out its core mission of bringing bluegrass friends together.

HOLLY BOND AND THE BLUEGRASS TEXANS

There's something about bluegrass music that touches your soul. It gets inside of you and makes you feel good.
—Holly Bond [38]

Mississippi, specifically the area near the Delta, is known for the genre of blues music. It yielded many of the greats, such as Charley Patton (considered to be the father of belta Blues), Robert Johnson and Big Bill Broonzy, among others. In 1934, it served as the birthplace of a boy who would go on to spend most of his life in Texas. He eventually made his mark on a style of music that wasn't common in either the Delta or the Lone Star State.

Holly Bond was born on June 18, 1934. From an early age, he was exposed to music, as most of his family played acoustic instruments. His father played guitar and harmonica, his uncle was a mandolinist and his grandfather was a fiddler. Bond also had a cousin who played resophonic-style (also known as dobro™) guitar on a standard Sears Roebuck model. The guitar was modified by placing the end of a toothbrush under the strings, allowing the guitar to be played in the same manner that early country players, such as Bashful Brother Oswald and Harold "Shot" Jackson, played.

While Holly was mostly exposed to country and bluegrass music in his early years, growing up in the Delta afforded him opportunities to be introduced to other styles of music. As a young boy, he got to know some other kids from New Orleans, Louisiana. They introduced him to the sounds of Cajun music, and Holly ultimately played some with them. Their instrumentation included instruments such as the fiddle and the accordion.

Holly Bond's 1972 album, *I Wonder*. *Standing*: Al Strebeck and Hunter Jones. *Kneeling*: Robert Grisham, Holly Bond and an unidentified fiddler. *Author's collection*.

Like many aspiring musicians, Bond also listened to recordings of other artists, including Bill Monroe, Flatt and Scruggs and Jimmy Martin. He also greatly admired the stylings of country singer Ernest Tubb, whose first hit song, "Walking the Floor Over You," would crossover into the pop music market in 1941.[39]

During Holly's teenage years, his father moved the family to Texas, as other members of his family had been living there for quite a while. They spent a brief period in Houston but eventually made their way to Arlington, Texas. In 1952, Bond entered the military during the Korean War.

Once Bond's time in the service ended, he returned to Arlington, where he eventually began working as a lieutenant for the Arlington Fire Department.

He was also playing music on the side, specializing in bluegrass and country music. In 1968, Holly met two men from Dallas who would become key figures in the next chapter of his musical journey. One was a police officer named Al Strebeck, and the other was a used car salesman by the name of Hunter Jones.

Strebeck and Jones encountered Bond's music and liked what they heard. They approached him with the idea of starting a group, but Strebeck was initially hesitant of because of his career with the fire department. The three men came to an agreement to maintain a part-time performance schedule for their new group. They soon started playing together and rehearsing material for their stage shows. As they were getting ready for their first performance, they still didn't have a name for this new band, an issue that was brought to light by a fiddler who joined the group shortly after their formation. As they were thinking of names, Holly remarked, "Well, we're Texans." Another member responded, "And we play bluegrass." As a result of these two remarks, the Bluegrass Texans were born. They quickly began playing shows around the Southwest.

The first recording by the Bluegrass Texans was the single "Make Me a Pallet On the Floor," accompanied by the band's rendition of the Bill Monroe song "I Haven't Seen Mary in Years" on the B side. Released on Holly Bond's self-owned Holly Records label in 1968, the single received airplay on Bill Mack's overnight *Country Roads Show* on WBAP, based in Fort Worth.[40]

In 1969, the group entered *The Original Amateur Hour*. The show, which began in 1934 as *Major Bowes' Amateur Hour*, was hosted by Major Edward Bowes and broadcast on the radio for nearly eleven years. It eventually moved to television in 1948 and was renamed *The Original Amateur Hour*. By this time, the show's host was broadcaster Ted Mack.[41] The show ran from 1948 to 1970 on various networks, with a brief revival in 1992. It is considered to be the precursor of televised talent competitions, such as *America's Got Talent* and *Star Search*. The Bluegrass Texans won the show, which would ultimately open more doors for them.

In the early 1970s, the Bluegrass Texans made their way to a studio in Hurst, Texas, to begin working on their first full-length album. The entire project was recorded in a single evening, with the session starting at 6:00 p.m. and ending at midnight. Holly and the band eagerly awaited the master recording so that they could move forward with releasing it, but they did not hear from their producer for weeks. This led to Bond and the Bluegrass Texans scheduling a second recording session with producer Bob Sullivan at Sumet Sound Studios in Dallas. Just two days before the band headed to Dallas, Holly received a call from their previous producer with some unfortunate news. The master tapes from their session in Hurst had been accidentally ruined by studio employees. The producer went ahead and sent the tapes to Bond in the hopes that some of the recordings could be potentially salvaged. Bob Sullivan at Sumet Sound concluded that only one song from the original session could be saved.

The group rerecorded the majority of the album at a session in Dallas. By this time, the Bluegrass Texans included Holly Bond on guitar, Hunter Jones on banjo, Al Strebeck on bass, Johnnie Luckie on fiddle and Robert Grisham on dobro. Mitchell Land of the Stone Mountain Boys contributed his mandolin playing to the recording as well. The end product, *I Wonder*, was released with Holly Records in 1972. The album contains several bluegrass standards, such as "My Walkin' Shoes" and "Pike County Breakdown," along with a few songs penned by Holly Bond, such as "I Wonder if You Think of Me at All" and "What About You." The final song on the recording, "Sally Goodin'," was taken from their first session in Hurst. Johnnie Luckie was not a member of the band at that time, and a different unidentified fiddler is playing on that track.

In 1973, the band got another wave of television exposure. Holly Bond happened to be in Fort Worth one day and decided to stop by Panther Hall in Fort Worth, a country music venue that was also home to the *Cowtown Jamboree*, a show that aired on Saturday evenings on KVT-TV.[42] After speaking with a security guard, Holly was allowed to meet with venue owner, Bill Kuykendall. He approached Kuykendall with the hopes of obtaining a guest spot for the Bluegrass Texans on the *Jamboree*. Bill agreed to audition the band the following week. That next Saturday, Holly Bond and the Bluegrass Texans arrived about thirty or forty minutes before that night's broadcast at Panther Hall. After hearing a couple of songs, Bill Kuykendall allowed them to open for that night's headliner. The thirty-minute performance they gave that evening resulted in the Bluegrass Texans being permanently hired to open the show every Saturday night moving forward. During this time, the band opened for several major stars, such as Jerry Lee Lewis, Dolly Parton and Hank Williams Jr.

The Bluegrass Texans had opportunities to open for other notable names outside of Panther Hall as well. One such instance was when Holly Bond received a call about opening for an act that had been booked to perform at East Texas State University. When Bond asked who the headliner was, the promoter informed him they would be opening for Ernest Tubb. This was a dream come true for Holly, as he had idolized Tubb since an early age. By this time, the Bluegrass Texans had also started playing the bluegrass festival circuit, which allowed them to cross paths with bluegrass pioneers, such as Bill Monroe, Lester Flatt, Jimmy Martin and Mac Wiseman. The group also served as the backing band for the legendary fiddlers Chubby Wise and Howdy Forrester, who had been scheduled to play a full set of twin fiddle music at Rod Kennedy's Bluegrass Festival in Kerrville, Texas, one year.

Throughout the group's thirty-five-year history, various musicians came through the ranks of the Bluegrass Texans, such as banjoist R.L. Johnson and mandolinist Richard Suddreth. One of the most interesting additions to the group was fiddler Verlon Stidham. Though he made his home in Chickasha, Oklahoma, he would drive eight or nine hours each way to meet up with the band at their personal appearances. Outside of the group's leader, Holly Bond, bassist Al Strebeck was the one constant member, remaining with the Bluegrass Texans for the entire run.

While the Bluegrass Texans primarily performed at events in the Southwest, the band would occasionally play in other states, such as Mississippi, Louisiana and Arkansas when the schedule allowed. They were one of only a few Texas-based bluegrass bands to have their own bus, which they referred to as Big Red.[43] In later years, they would travel in a motor home.

The Bluegrass Texans recorded several more projects on CD and cassette formats. Some of them were studio albums, and others were live recordings, captured at different events the band played. The group's final recording was a gospel release. Holly Bond's mother had always wanted him to record an album of all gospel material, so this was his way of fulfilling that wish. By this time, the group consisted of Bond on guitar, Al Strebeck on bass, Eddie Green on mandolin and Wayne Harris on banjo.

After retiring from the Arlington Fire Department as a fire captain and EMT coordinator, Holly opened Holly Bond Music in Paris, Texas, a music store that also housed a recording studio. This is where the Bluegrass Texans recorded some of their later projects. He would run this business for eighteen years. In 2009, Bond sold the business that would ultimately be renamed Rockin' L Music and Recording.

JOHNNIE MARTIN AND THE BLUEGRASS RAMBLERS OF TEXAS

Although he lived most of his life in the Lone Star State and most of his musical pursuits occurred there, Johnnie Morgan Martin was born on April 14, 1931, in Louisiana, where he lived for much of his early years, along with his mother, father and three brothers.[44] He began playing music in his early teens.

In 1953, Martin moved to Wiergate, Texas, near the Beaumont area. He and his wife, Ann, would make their home there for several decades. It also served as the place where they raised their three children. It's not certain exactly when Johnnie started playing music in the area, but in 1962, he formed the Bluegrass Ramblers of Texas.[45] Martin was the group's lead singer and guitarist.

The band would ultimately perform shows on a local and regional basis. They also made several appearances on both radio and television. In August 1970, shortly after performing at Bill Grant's Bluegrass Festival in Hugo, Oklahoma, the Bluegrass Ramblers made their way to Austin, Texas, where they purchased their own bus. Despite the vehicle needing some repairs (specifically a new engine that the band members helped install), it was the first of several milestones the group would achieve.[46]

The next step in their semiprofessional journey would come in 1972, when the Bluegrass Ramblers of Texas released their first album, *Bluegrass Music from Bluebonnet Country*, with Dane Records, based out of Houston. The project was produced by label owner, Ray Doggett, and it was recorded at his independently owned Doggett Sound Studios. By this time, the band included Martin on guitar, mandolinist Kenneth Clemons, fiddler Kenneth Holder and eighteen-year-old banjoist Jim Moratto. As the album was being recorded, the group's regular bassist, James Clemons, was serving in the air force. As a result, Emil Humbert of Groesbeck, Texas, was brought in to play bass. Fiddler Bill Northcutt was also brought in to play twin fiddle with Kenneth Holder on a few songs. Dane Records also released a single that featured the songs "Indian Hollow" and "This Last Request."

Soon after this, the Ramblers scored a really big break. Rod Kennedy, the promoter of the Kerrville Folk Festival, had heard of the Bluegrass Ramblers of Texas, as they had been mentioned to him by several festival attendees who felt there needed to be a bluegrass band on the lineup. He eventually saw them perform at a bluegrass festival and ultimately booked them to perform at the 1973 event, making them the first-ever bluegrass band to

The Bluegrass Ramblers of Texas at the Kerrville Bluegrass Festival in September 1974. *From left to right*: Randy Morgan, Kenneth Holder, Kenneth Clemmons, Johnnie Martin and James Hicks. *Photograph courtesy of Rick Gardner.*

appear on the bill.[47] At the time of this performance, the Bluegrass Ramblers of Texas were made up of most of the same musicians who appeared on *Bluegrass Music from Bluebonnet Country*, with the exception of James Hicks on bass. Their performance from that weekend was professionally recorded and subsequently released as *"Live" at the Kerrville Folk Festival*. The album was produced by Rod Kennedy and Pedro Gutierrez. Shortly after this, banjoist Jim Moratto left the Bluegrass Ramblers of Texas to join Bill Monroe and the Bluegrass Boys. He was Monroe's regular banjoist from 1973 to 1974 and even appeared with the band on the *Lester Flatt Live Bluegrass Festival* album from RCA Records.

The Bluegrass Ramblers of Texas continued to perform at regional bluegrass festivals and other local events. They also had a standing engagement to perform at the Kerrville Folk Festival every year. In 1975, the band released a third studio recording. Unfortunately, not much is known about this particular project. In the late 1970s, Johnnie Martin's health began to deteriorate, but he was determined to keep the group going.

In January 1982, the Bluegrass Ramblers of Texas recorded their final album, *Travelin' Man*, at Ludwig Sound Recording Studios in Houston. Along with Martin on guitar and Kenneth Holder on fiddle, the final configuration of the Ramblers consisted of Marvin Hutchins on banjo, John Tiekle on lead guitar, Steve Moore on bass and a teenager named Russell Moore on mandolin. Russell quickly showed potential as a lead and tenor vocalist. On *Travelin' Man*, Moore sings lead on six of the twelve songs. He also contributed harmony vocals and played some bass on the album's other tracks.

Shortly after *Travelin' Man* was released, the Bluegrass Ramblers of Texas officially disbanded. While this was largely due to Johnnie Martin's declining health, another factor was the departure of Russell Moore, who had decided to form a band with Scott Vestal called Southern Connection.[48]

In 1983, one year after the Bluegrass Ramblers of Texas disbanded, Johnnie Martin retired from his day job as a machinist for the Shell Chemical Company. It was some time after this that he and his wife, Ann, returned to his native Louisiana. They resided in the small town of Pitkin. Johnnie Martin lived there until his passing on April 19, 1995, at the age of sixty-four.[49]

RUSSELL MOORE

Russell Moore was born on December 21, 1963. Growing up in Pasadena, Texas, Moore first heard bluegrass music around the age of seven or eight, when he attended a bluegrass show with some family members. He quickly fell in love with the genre. In his early years, Russell's strongest influence was the Osborne Brothers, particularly the singing of Bobby Osborne, whose high vocal range gave the group it's distinct identity.

By the time he was eleven years old, Moore began learning how to play various instruments, such as the mandolin and the bass. At the age of fifteen, he joined Johnnie Martin and the Bluegrass Ramblers of Texas. During this time, he honed his ability as a lead and tenor vocalist. He stayed with the group until 1982.

At the age of eighteen, Russell moved to Arlington, Texas, to form the band Southern Connection with banjoist Scott Vestal. While there, the band recorded the self-titled album *Southern Connection*. Shortly after this, the entire group moved to North Carolina in order to further their musical career.

Not long after their relocation, the group received a call from Doyle Lawson. He had heard Southern Connection when they opened a show for him and his band, Quicksilver, in Tarkington, Texas. Lawson was impressed by what he heard, particularly Russell's high vocal range. Doyle recruited Moore to play guitar and sing lead and tenor vocals, along with Scott Vestal on banjo and baritone vocals and his brother Curtis Vestal on bass and bass

Russell Moore. *Photograph courtesy of East Public Relations.*

vocals. Russell was a member of Doyle Lawson and Quicksilver for six years. During that time, he appeared on seven of the band's recordings.

In 1991, Moore, along with bassist Ray Deaton and fiddler Mike Hartgrove, left Doyle Lawson and Quicksilver to form the band IIIrd Tyme Out. The group went on to receive numerous accolades, including being named vocal group of the year by the IBMA from 1994 to 2000. Russell was also awarded male vocalist of the year in 1994, 1997, 2010, 2011, 2012 and 2018. In 2007, the band was rebranded as Russell Moore and IIIrd Tyme Out.[50]

JOE BASS AND THE DOUBLE MOUNTAIN BOYS

On September 20, 1932, in a tiny northeast Louisiana town called Ivan, Joe Franklin Bass was born to James and Hattie Bass. It's unclear when the Bass family made their way to Texas, but Joe did graduate from Lipan High School.

Bass had played some music in his early years, but he didn't start learning how to play the guitar until he served with the army during the Korean War. On November 7, 1953, he married Barbara Arthur in Palo Pinto County.[51] They made their home in Lipan, Texas, which is located in Hood County.

In 1960, Joe, along with banjoist Noel Ownbey, guitarists David Addison and Charles Stewart, bassist Jeff Miller and fiddler Bill Northcutt, formed a band. The group's name, the Double Mountain Boys, would ultimately be coined by Ownbey, paying homage to two small mountains in Palo Pinto County.[52]

Although the group released many recordings during their time together, their first studio album, *The Bluegrass Sounds of the Double Mountain Boys*, was released eight years after their initial formation. Released with the Fort Worth–based Bluebonnet Recording Studios label, this recording showcased the group performing several bluegrass standards, such as "Uncle Pen," "Roll in My Sweet Baby's Arms" and "Muleskinner Blues." By this time, the group included Tommy Hughes on fiddle and his brother Johnny on rhythm guitar, along with Bass, Ownbey and Stewart.

The 1970s proved to be a particularly notable decade for the Double Mountain Boys. In 1972, they performed at the first annual Glen Rose Bluegrass Jamboree Festival in Glen Rose, Texas, an event that the group would continue to perform at every year until October 2017.[53]

In March 1973, they met bluegrass pioneer Robert Russell "Chubby" Wise.[54] By this time, Wise had relocated to Livingston, Texas, which is close to Huntsville. Wise began a working relationship with the group, contributing his fiddle playing to a few of their recordings, as well as writing liner notes for their second studio recording, *The Double Mountain Boys at the Blue Ridge Cabin Home*, which was released in 1975. In May 1973, the Double Mountain Boys were among several groups to perform at the first annual Mayfest in Fort Worth, Texas, an event that has had an attendance of 200,000 people.[55]

As with many bands, the Double Mountain Boys had different musicians come and go throughout their history. Some of those players included fiddler Johnnie Luckie, bassist Charlie McCurdy, resonator guitarist Kenneth Addison (brother of original member David Addison) and mandolinist Ray Boyer. Throughout the 1970s and 1980s, the group continued making studio recordings. Although the band always employed bluegrass-style instrumentation, the Double Mountain Boys' sound eventually became more reminiscent of classic country music. The earliest recorded example of this was an album titled *A Tribute to Hank Williams*, which was self-released by the band on their own Double Mountain Records label. Although the year of this project's release is unknown, it was more than likely recorded between the early and mid-1970s, as evidenced by the fiddle playing of Chubby Wise and the contributions of Joe Bass, Noel Ownbey, Kenneth Addison and his brother David, who, by this point, had returned to the band after a brief hiatus.

The final configuration of the Double Mountain Boys. *From left to right*: Slick Gilmore, Jimmy Walker, Jerry Watts and Joe Bass. *Photograph courtesy of the* Hood County News.

The Double Mountain Boys continued to perform and record for several more decades. In 1999, Jimmy Walker of Granbury, Texas, joined the band on rhythm guitar and vocals. Although he didn't become a Double Mountain Boy until decades into their existence, Walker's friendship with Joe Bass dates back to the early 1950s, when they both attended Lipan High School. The two lost contact once Bass graduated, but the friendship was eventually rekindled when both men started running into each other at various bluegrass festivals.[56]

In 2002, the Double Mountain Boys released two CDs titled *By Special Request Volume I* and *Volume II*. These projects contained many country classics that had originally been recorded by legendary artists, such as Webb Pierce, Merle Haggard, Eddy Arnold and Marty Robbins. For a number of years, Joe Bass ran two bluegrass festivals in Stephenville, Texas, the last one being held in May 2004.[57]

Although the group released its seventeenth and final recording in 2009, the band continued performing sporadically until Joe Bass became ill in early 2019. He passed away a few months later, on April 7, at the age of eighty-six. The final configuration of the Double Mountain Boys consisted of Bass and Jimmy Walker on guitar, Slick Gilmore on resophonic guitar and Jerry Watts on bass.

4

THE 1970s, '80s AND '90s

By the time the 1970s rolled around, bluegrass music was beginning to have more of a presence within the Lone Star State. More bands were starting to emerge, such as Ronnie Gill's Bluegrass Kinfolks, the Tennessee Valley Authority and Hickory Hill, among others.

Another contributing factor was the addition of the country and bluegrass music associate degree to South Plains College music program in Levelland, as well as the foundation of the Central Texas Bluegrass Association in Austin.

While all of this was happening, several Texans, such as Danny Barnes, Karl Shiflett, Lynn Morris and Marshall Wilborn, were busy honing their craft. By the 1990s, all of these Texans would go on to have successful music careers in their own right, bringing their brands of bluegrass music to audiences all over the United States and beyond.

A Bluegrass College in West Texas

The city of Levelland is in far west Texas, thirty miles west of Lubbock and forty miles east of the New Mexico border. This little town his home to South Plains College, where bluegrass has been cultivated since 1975.

In the early 1970s Nathan Tubb was the academic dean at South Plains College. Nathan could not figure out why students were not signing up for music classes. One semester, he spent three days at registration, with a yellow legal pad, interviewing students.

Left: Alan Munde (*left*) and Joe Carr, Houston, Texas, December 6, 1986, *Two Swell Guys from West Texas*. *Photograph courtesy of Rick Gardner.*

Below: South Plains College in Levelland, Texas. *Photograph courtesy of Brandon L. Magnano.*

For the most part, the questions and answers went like this: "Are you signing up for band?" *No.* "Did you play in the high school band?" *Yes.* "Why don't you want to be in band now?" *It's not fun.* "Do you like music?" *Yes.*

The students told Nathan that they wanted to play guitar, fiddle, steel guitar, banjo or sing in a band.

Nathan took this information to the school president, who told him to hire a guitar teacher. In 1974, Nathan took out an advertisement in *Country Music Roundup* magazine. At about the same time, in Nebraska, Patty Hartin bought her husband, John, a subscription to *Country Roundup Magazine.*

John Hartin, a musical instrument salesman for Conn Music and a professional guitarist, was thumbing through the latest issue of *Country Music Roundup*. He noticed an advertisement from a school in West Texas that wanted to hire a guitar teacher.

Soon, John found himself on a plane heading to Lubbock, Texas. Nathan Tubb picked John up at the airport, and they headed to Levelland to tour the campus. After the tour, Nathan invited John to his house and asked him to play a few tunes.

The following day, there was a two-hour interview at the college, and John was offered the job. John left his lucrative position at Conn Music and moved into his tiny office, located in the South Plains College Women's Gym.

In 1976, Nathan Tubb and John Hartin launched a new program: an associate degree in country music. John was a natural salesman, sending letters to magazines and writing articles in praise of the program. The number of enrolled students grew, and the degree name was changed to "country and bluegrass" as part of the Commercial Music Program.

As the program grew, in 1978, two instructors were hired to serve the students' needs: West Texan Tim McCasland and fiddler extraordinaire Ed Marsh. Ed and John took a few student ensembles to the South Plains Fair in Lubbock. The fair gave the students an opportunity to gain experience playing in front of a live audience while also providing publicity for the school.

The fair also featured major country music acts, such as Johnny Cash, Charlie Pride and Tom T. Hall. Knowing Tom T. Hall loved bluegrass music, Ed Marsh invited him to visit the school. Hall was so impressed that he later brought a film crew to South Plains College and filmed a short documentary on the country and bluegrass music program. The piece was included in Tom T. Hall's 1979 bluegrass special on PBS. The television exposure resulted in further growth. The school's relationship with Tom T. Hall also flourished.

In 1987, Hall returned to South Plains College and led "the World's Largest Bluegrass Band." The band consisted of over two hundred musicians of all ages. Proceeds from the concert established the Tom T. and Dixie Hall Scholarship Fund. The concert was held in conjunction with the opening of the Tom T. Hall Recording and Production Studio. Over the years, the studio stage has been a musical platform for professional musicians, such as Joe Bonamasa, Eric Johnson, Chuck Rainey, Marcia Ball, Tony Trischka and Ron Block.

The studio opened next to a recording studio named for Waylon Jennings. In 1980, the college added a sound technology degree and built a sixteen-

SPC First To Offer Country Music Degree

By GERRY BURTON
Avalanche-Journal Staff

LEVELLAND — "Let me have an E," he says, and the sounds come back from electric, steel and standard guitars, mixed with a few voices.

Then, he pats one foot and swings the other while his own fingers tickle a guitar.

It's country and western music time at South Plains College, the only school in the world putting the country and western and bluegrass music into classrooms toward a degree.

"Now let's try" and "let's blend a little steel in here" language usually found at a jam session is a part of the SPC classroom terminology, part of a program gaining national attention for the junior college.

SPC bandsmen will be bringing their country sound, in growing demand around the South Plains, to open house festivities at Reese Air Force Base on Monday, swinging out at 1 p.m.

Teacher for the music segment of the bluegrass as well as the country and western associate degree requirements is John Hartin of Norfolk, Neb., who was writing country music at nine and performing with his own band at 14.

Hartin, a veteran of many years of road shows and backing up name performers on the guitar, came to SPC after seeing an advertisement for a college bluegrass teacher in a country and western magazine.

The ad was the final step in several years of preparation to get the sound into the classroom, a program pioneered by Nathan Tubb, SPC academic dean.

"We are today where I figured we'd be in three years," Tubb said as the program moved into its second year with 14 majors and a few others leaning toward country music as a major.

With the sound grabbing young minds, filling prime entertainment time and drawing tens of thousands to festivals, Tubb felt it SPC's duty — "as a commun-

ity college obligated to accommodate what the community wants to learn" — to offer the music.

A few years ago he was making arrangements for students to use vacant classrooms to jam a little in spare time. Next, he was looking seriously into the idea of bringing the shade tree variety of instruction up to the college level and "above the picking and grinning" stage.

Three years ago SPC offered guitar lessons in evening class.

"More turned up than the teacher could handle — teenagers, housewives, teachers, senior citizens, businessmen — we had to make three sections instead of one," Tubb said.

"It confirmed my suspicion that people wanted to learn bluegrass and country and western."

First, he had to win approval of the college and instructors of traditional music.

Next, he had to find the right instructor, one who could work in a college environment, but also be a fine musician in this day and time.

Hartin, who had stopped road work long enough to get a degree in business administration from Briar Cliff College in Iowa, fit the qualifications.

He can teach in several hours, he said, things it took him months to learn by trial and error.

Basic instruction in music and theory is combined with country and western arranging and a working knowledge of how to perform.

"We try to keep the shade tree concept even in the classroom," Hartin said, noting music was not available and that teaching by showing and by record was a necessary part of country music, as it always had been.

Students get concentrated amounts of proven methods tailor made to classrooms where the "swapping of licks" is fined down to solid instruction based on musical knowledge of traditional ways.

The program grows with the spreading of the word about a college teaching what many youngsters want to learn, for a sideline or a career.

Examples include Tim McCasland of Lubbock, who backed off on an English major after his junior year at Texas Tech to see if he could get better on his guitar and wound up going great on the banjo. He came for one semester and will end with three before returning to Tech for his degree in English.

Toby Hise of Haskell always wanted to be in country music, heard about the program and is working out his own unique singing and playing style.

B Local Family News **METRO**

Lubbock Avalanche-Journal   Thursday, Oct. 7, 1976

College celebrates Tom T. Hall Day

LEVELLAND, Texas (AP) — Country music star Tom T. Hall joined nearly 200 musicians from across the country at South Plains College for some down-home pickin' to help dedicate a music studio in his name.

Hall, 50, helped celebrate Tom T. Hall Day on Thursday and dedicated the Tom T. Hall Recording and Production studio, a unique facility where students can

learn about country and bluegrass music, said college spokeswoman Dianne Lawson.

"He visited the campus in 1979 and we have a two-year program in country and bluegrass music," she said. "He filmed some footage for a PBS special back in 1979, and then the publicity from that kind of helped the growth of the program."

Hall joined about 185 other musi-

cians for a special concert Thursday.

"We had all kinds of pickers — guitars, banjos, mandolins and fiddles," Ms. Lawson said. "It was all led by Tom T. Hall and also his band played too, the Storytellers."

He later received an honorary associate of arts degree in country and bluegrass music, she said.

South Plains College has over 3,000 students on three campuses.

Top: South Plains College. *From "First to Offer Country Music Degree,"* Lubbock Avalanche Journal, *October 7, 1976.*

Bottom: Tom T. Hall Day at Levelland College. *From* Paris News, *March 27, 1987.*

---

track recording studio. Waylon Jennings's son, Buddy, enrolled in the program. Waylon came out to Levelland to visit Buddy and to learn more about the program.

During his visit, John Hartin and Waylon went across the street to the Dairy Queen for lunch. Jennings, who had been a young DJ in his native Arizona, told John he wished something like this had been available to him. As the conversation continued, Waylon asked John how he could help.

John told Waylon that they were always in need of funding. Waylon said he would bring the band and hold a concert to raise funds. The demand for tickets was so great that the concert had to be moved to the coliseum in Lubbock. John Hartin said, "Waylon donated everything to the school. He

The Tom T. Hall Production Studio. *Photograph courtesy of Brandon L. Magnano.*

didn't even charge expenses."[58] The school named the recording studio in Waylon's honor. Waylon and his wife, Jessie Colter, also donated a Kawai grand piano to the recording studio.[59]

As the school continued to grow in the 1980s, the faculty also grew in number and status. John Hartin hired two of the most accomplished bluegrass musicians in the world: Joe Carr and Alan Munde. Carr and Munde raised the program's profile, and South Plains began to attract students from all over the world. Many of these students grew up listening to Carr and Munde and were thrilled to learn from their bluegrass heroes.

Denton native Joe Carr, a phenomenal musician, proficient on mandolin, guitar and fiddle, began teaching at South Plains College in 1984. Joe was hired as the "bluegrass specialist." Joe had played with the band Roanoke in the 1970s and with the highly acclaimed Country Gazette in the 1970s and 1980s.

Just how did he end up in Levelland?

> *Gazette played there at the college in '83. We did a concert and a small workshop, and then the Gazette played there in early '84 without me, after*

*I had left, and essentially they went, "Where is that guy?" So, Alan called
me within a week and said, "They are looking to expand their faculty and
understand you are available, so why don't you give them a call." I was
back in Dallas, teaching lessons and sort of doing what I could to make a
living off of the road. So, I called them and wound up going to work for
them in mid-'84.*[60]

Joe taught at South Plains College for thirty years and spent many years as
the director of "Camp Bluegrass," a one-week summer camp for bluegrass
musicians. Joe lived with multiple sclerosis for many years and passed away
from a stroke in 2014.

Banjo virtuoso Alan Munde (Stone Mountain Boys, Flying Burrito
Brothers, Jimmy Martin), Joe's Country Gazette bandmate, was hired by
the college in 1984. Alan shared his banjo knowledge and skills in Levelland
until he retired in 2002.

John Hartin was inducted into the West Texas Walk of Fame in 1998.

*The West Texas Walk of Fame honors those individuals/groups with a strong
connection to Lubbock and the West Texas area who have devoted a significant
part of their lives to the development and production of the performing and*

Texas flag autographed guitar by South Plains College alum Lee Ann Womack. Lee Ann
would place eleven singles in the Country Music Top Twenty after leaving SPC. *Photograph
courtesy of Brandon L. Magnano.*

John Hartin, the man who built the program at South Plains College, at his store, Texas Music Supply, in Levelland, Texas. *Photograph courtesy of Brandon L. Magnano.*

visual arts and whose body of work has been influential nationally in one of more of these areas. The West Texas area, for the purposes of this project, is generally interpreted as a 150-mile radius of Lubbock.[61]

Other inductees include Buddy Holly, Waylon Jennings, Joe Ely, the Maines Brothers Band and Mac Davis.

In 2003, John retired as the chairman and professor of music at South Plains College. He said, "I felt everything was in good hands and the school had a bright future. I did what I wanted to do—build a world class program."[62] But a builder keeps building; John is the co-owner of Texas Music Supply, and since 1975, he has played guitar for the Hot Texas Band. John is also a member of both the Nebraska Rock and Roll Hall of Fame and the Iowa Rock and Roll Hall of Fame. Who remembers the Teen Beats?

After John retired, Cary C. Banks became the new Creative Arts Department chairperson, a position he would hold until he retired in 2016. Cary started teaching at the college in 1993 for what he thought would be a one-semester deal. A longtime member of the Maines Brothers Band, Cary has also been inducted into the West Texas Walk of Fame.

Cary started out teaching piano and voice at the college, but he also continued building on the program's foundation. John Hartin asked Cary to develop a student showcase, incorporating sound and video. Cary conceptualized and implemented the department's *Thursday Night Live* television show. The show was broadcast on the college's television station and continues to this day.

Cary was then promoted to program coordinator of the Commercial Music Program before taking over for John. Since retiring from his role as chairperson, Cary has written a book, *Almost Like a Professional: My Life and Career as a West Texas Musician*, and released a CD of piano instrumentals titled, fittingly, *Piano*.

The Commercial Music Program at South Plains College has grown to encompasses ensembles in bluegrass, country, rock, jazz and western swing. Private lessons are given in guitar, bass, mandolin, banjo, fiddle, dobro, pedal steel guitar, drums, voice, piano and keyboards.

Many talented musicians have spent time studying at South Plains College. The following is a list of some of the most distinguished South Plains College alumni:

- Cody Angel: steel guitar (Jason Boland and the Stragglers)
- Ron Block: singer/songwriter, banjo, guitar (Alison Krause and Union Station)
- Ashley Brown: fiddle
- Mike Bub: upright bass
- Ben Clark: songwriter, guitar, banjo, mandolin, dobro and piano
- Katy and Penny Clark: (the Purple Hulls)
- Stuart Duncan: fiddle, mandolin, guitar and banjo
- Jeremy Garrett: fiddle (the Infamous Stringdusters)
- Nate Lee: mandolin
- Natalie Maines: lead singer, songwriter (the Chicks)
- Jeremy Moyers: steel guitar
- Jerrod Nieman: songwriter
- Erin and Amber Rogers: (Scenic Routes)
- Amanda Shires: fiddle, singer/songwriter
- Craig Smith: Scottish guitarist
- Ricky Turpin: fiddle (Asleep at the Wheel)
- Kym Warner: vocals, mandolin (the Greencards)
- Lee Ann Womack: singer
- Heath Wright: lead singer, guitarist (Ricochet)

Lonnie Joe Howell, co-owner of Texas Music Supply with John Hartin, is also a South Plains College alum. A master of the harmonica, Lonnie has released three harmonica instructional DVDs and four albums, including 2020's *Happy, Texas*.

Lonnie graduated from Texas Tech and taught math for six years—then the music bug bit. He attended South Plains from 1978 to 1980. After finishing his associate degree, he enrolled in Nashville's Belmont College (now

Belmont University) and graduated with a bachelor's degree in commercial music. This is what Lonnie had to say about his South Plains experience: "Between classes, there were jams. Everywhere you look, someone was pickin' under a tree, in a hallway or a dorm room. Teachers would jam with students and remembered everybody's name. Positivity was encouraged; it was a totally connected, shared passion"[63]

RONNIE GILL AND THE BLUEGRASS KINFOLKS

When Earl Scruggs began performing with Bill Monroe in 1945, many people found themselves drawn to his rapid three-finger banjo picking style. Pretty soon, many would begin learning the instrument themselves. Many of those aspiring banjoists, such as Ronnie Gill from the Abilene area, would find themselves on a relentless quest to duplicate this exciting new sound.

Ronnie found himself drawn to the banjo, particularly the style pioneered by Earl Scruggs. His grandfather from Alabama specialized in the frailing style (also known as clawhammer) of banjo playing that had been popularized by Grandpa Jones, David "Stringbean" Akeman and Uncle Dave Macon, among others. Gill knew that he needed a five-string banjo like his grandfather in order to play. His biggest challenge, however, was finding someone who could teach him all the nuances of Scruggs's style. Ronnie sought out the help of local musicians to help him learn. While they did show him variations of three-finger-style banjo playing, Gill found himself unsatisfied, as, to his ears, it did not sound anything like what he heard Scruggs play. Eventually, he was able to get pointers from Bill Emerson, a Washington, D.C.–based banjoist who performed with numerous bluegrass artists, such as Jimmy Martin, Cliff Waldron and the Country Gentlemen.[64]

Ronnie, along with Carl Fitzgerald, formed the Bluegrass Kinfolks in 1965. Even as the group was developing it's sound, Ronnie was able to further his study of the banjo. In 1968, he got the opportunity to see Bill Monroe and the Bluegrass Boys in Big Spring, Texas. After the performance, Ronnie received informal instruction from Monroe's banjoist at the time, Vic Jordan. The next year, Gill attended Monroe's third annual Bluegrass Festival in Bean Blossom, Indiana, where he was able to observe many different players and learn even more about Scruggs-style banjo.

By the late 1960s, the Bluegrass Kinfolks were incredibly active. At this point, the group consisted of Ronnie on banjo; Fitzgerald on lead guitar;

Gill's wife, Ann, on bass; their daughter Debbie on mandolin; Ann Dye on rhythm guitar; and Ansel Shupe on mandolin. In 1969, the group won first place in two different band contests—one at the Peachtree Festival in DeLeon, Texas, and another in Snyder, Texas, where they competed against eighteen other bands. Debbie Gill also won first place in the junior mandolin contest that was held at Bill Grant's Bluegrass Festival in Hugo, Oklahoma. She won this competition again the next year, in 1970.[65]

In 1972, Gill won first place in the banjo contest that was held at the first annual Glen Rose Bluegrass Jamboree. In 1975, the Bluegrass Kinfolks released their only album, *Big Country Bluegrass.* By this time, the band consisted of Ron, Debbie and Ann Gill, Carl Fitzgerald, fiddler Bill Burns and rhythm guitarist Robert Boyd. During that time, the Bluegrass Kinfolks had their own fifteen-minute segment on a weekly country radio show called the *Saturday Afternoon Shindig*, which aired on KTSA in Coleman, Texas. Gill also hosted his own radio show at a station in a little town west of Abilene called Merkel.

In 1976, Ronnie hosted the first annual Buffalo Gap Bluegrass Festival, making it the first bluegrass-related event to ever be held in West Texas. Although the Bluegrass Kinfolks were eventually disbanded, Gill would continue to be active in bluegrass music. He went on to form a new band, Buffalo Gap Bluegrass, which included Bill Burns and Robert Boyd. He also continued to host the Buffalo Gap Bluegrass Festival, which ran consecutively from 1976 to 1988.

In August 2013, Gill hosted a new version of his event called Ronnie Gill's Bluegrass Festival. Along with performances by Ronnie and Bill Burns, the lineup consisted of solely Texas-based talent, such as Joe Bass and the Double Mountain Boys and Concho Grass, among others.[66]

SAN ANTONIO'S TENNESSEE VALLEY AUTHORITY

Hank Harrison has kept the flag flying for bluegrass in Texas.[67]
—*Peter Rowan*

If you use a search engine and type in "Tennessee Valley Authority," you will find link after link about the federally owned corporation started in 1933 by President Franklin D. Roosevelt. The TVA provides economic development, electricity, recreation, navigation and flood control for the Tennessee River Valley.

Hank Harrison (*left*) with Peter Rowan.
Photograph courtesy of Rick Gardner.

You will have to add "bluegrass band" to "Tennessee Valley Authority" to your search to locate the San Antonio bluegrass band that was started in 1972. So, how did a band from San Antonio come up with a name associated with Tennessee? Why did they not name themselves the "Comal River Boys," "the Black Hill Boys" or "San Antonio River Boys?" Hank Harrison said:

> *At first, we were going for a Texas-oriented name. Then we decided to choose a name from where the music started: Kentucky, Tennessee. We noticed a lot of bluegrass bands had valley or mountain in their names. We chose Tennessee Valley Authority; figured they wouldn't mind if we use it.*[68]

Which brings us to our next question: how did teenagers in San Antonio, Texas, become interested in bluegrass music? According to Hank Harrison:

> *My brother Jeff and I were in high school, and we worked for a friend who ran a flea market. He heard that there was another flea market opening up in a western village* [movie set]. *He wanted to know which of our dealers was setting up over there, so he sent us to do a little detective work. When we got there, they had a live bluegrass band playing on the boardwalk* [the Backwoods Volunteers]. *Jeff and I both played a little guitar, but we had never seen a live bluegrass band before, and we were gobsmacked! We did our detective work, but we couldn't get that band out of our minds. So, when we got back to our flea market, we told all the dealers that we were looking for bluegrass instruments. The next week, one dealer brought a dobro* [acoustic steel guitar], *and another brought a fiddle! We both thought that the dobro was cool, and we both knew that the fiddle was*

difficult, so we flipped a coin, and I lost the toss. That was in 1971, and now, today, forty-seven years later, we both still play the instruments that flipped nickel picked out for us![69]

My dad and mom were both commercial artists. They taught us to draw, and they taught us to pick. My mom played tenor guitar and mandolin. My dad played guitar. My grandmother played piano. She used to play for silent movies. Our next door neighbor played guitar. My parents had jam sessions at the house. They played country and blues. After Jeff and I started playing together, my dad said we should find something for my youngest brother, Scott. Somebody brought a bass fiddle into the flea market. We got it for Scott and told him we had a gig in two days. He learned to play bass.[70]

We started in 1972 with the Tennessee Valley Authority bluegrass band [with Mark Maniscalco on banjo*]; *our second choice for a band name was Johnson Grass! The TVA won its first band contest in 1980 in Kerrville and went on to win three other Texas contests before taking on the biggest and most prestigious national band contest in Louisville, Kentucky, in 1984. We won big bucks, a recording session with the legendary Sam Bush and extensive bragging rights.*[71]

The TVA has opened shows for the Dixie Chicks (now known as the Chicks), Ralph Stanley, Michael Martin Murphy, Alan Munde and the Country Gazette, Tony Trischka, Hot Rize, Tony Rice, Doyle Lawson and Quicksilver and the Del McCoury Band. They have also toured with Peter Rowan, Jerry Douglas and Kenny Baker and performed with guitar virtuoso Junior Brown, the father of bluegrass Bill Monroe and the king of the accordion Flaco Jimenez.

The TVA has also been involved in local charities and historic preservation efforts. Kathy Hill, the president of the Leon Valley Historic Society, said:

[Oh, my God], *TVA has been a tremendous supporter of the Leon Valley Historical Society and especially our efforts to preserve and restore the Huebner-Onion Homestead and Stagecoach. They have provided*

---

* Mark Maniscalco would go on to win the Winfield, Kansas National Banjo Championship in 1975, turn down Bill Monroe's offer to be a Bluegrass Boy because he didn't want to travel, play banjo with the San Antonio Symphony Orchestra, release a banjo instructional LP and record with Carol King on her *Pearls Time Gone By* album.

entertainment at the majority of our events and have been vocal in the community and area, supporting us. Hank has been our contact and good friend over the years.[72]

Through many personnel changes, Hank Harrison has been the anchor. The band was still going strong in 2020.

KERRVILLE'S POVERTY PLAYBOYS

But I know that your bunch—the cute thing about it was—it was kind of hard times back in some of those days. So, they came up with a neat idea of being Poverty Playboys. So, they dressed in their overalls and their beat-up hats and loud shirts and everything, so it went over. It was always a popular, popular thing.
—Clarabelle Snodgrass, interviewing the Poverty Playboys' Clyde Jones[73]

The Poverty Playboys were founded by a radio station owner, featured a retired judge as their lead singer, the judge's wife played upright bass, a hospital superintendent played guitar and, for a while, a Texas ranger (not the baseball kind) was in the band.

Judge Robert "Bob" Rhea Barton had learned to play a baritone ukulele tuned like a tenor banjo while attending college at Schreiner Institute (Schreiner University). Clyde Jones owned Kerrville's KERV radio station and was also a musician, proficient on guitar, fiddle and mandolin. Bob and Clyde met, and Bob was asked to play on the radio.

Clyde Jones formed the bluegrass-gospel band Poverty Playboys in 1967. The band consisted Clyde and Bob, Kerrville State Hospital superintendent Luther Ross on guitar and Ken McCormick on bass. The band's membership was a revolving door over the years. Judge Bob Barton said, "We had Ed Gooding, a Texas ranger, play with us for a while, too." In 1980, Joyce Barton (Bob's wife) took over on bass; Howard Walker brought his "5" (string banjo), mandolin and lead guitar; and Clay took up the rhythm guitar.[74]

The band played locally for almost forty years. They played during halftime at Schreiner Mountaineer football games (Schreiner no longer fields a team as of this writing), the Kerrville Bluegrass Festival, churches, various charity events, retirement homes, the VA, sheep dippings and graveyard workings.[75]

The band recorded only one album, 2004's *Take Your Shoes Off Moses*. The Poverty Playboys played their last show in 2005.

GRASSFIRE

The Austin-based band Grassfire actually started out as the Texas Bluegrass Boys. Band leader Jim Barr (mandolin) had moved from South Carolina to Austin in 1949. He founded the Texas Bluegrass Boys in 1953. The band also featured Leo Campbell, Lonnie Leighton and Harold Franks (banjo).

When Barr's daughter Sherri joined the band on guitar, they changed their name to Grassfire. In 1974, the band added Leonard Kasza on dobro.

The band recorded two albums during their time together. Their album from 1978, *Bluegrass to Walk On*, featured covers of standards, such "Precious Memories"; originals written by Jim Barr; and the title song, which was written by Jim and Sherri Barr. Their last album was *Grassfire's Family Reunion*, released in 1982. *Family Reunion* comprised another mix of standards and originals, with four songs composed by Sherrie Barr.

Another high point for the band was a tour of Mexico that occurred over ten days in July 1981. The tour was through the "Partners of the Americas" program, with joint sponsorship from the Mexican and United

GRASSFIRE, FROM AUSTIN, will be one of the groups providing entertainment at Rod Kennedy's 7th Annual Bluegrass Festival in Kerrville. The Festival is set for August 28-31. Members of the group include Jim Barr, Sherri Barr, Harold Franks, John Kubecka and Bobby Lee Roberts.

Grassfire promotion for the 1980 Kerrville Bluegrass Festival. *From the* Waco Citizen, *August 22, 1980.*

Grassfire appearing with Cedar Ridge and Southern Select at the Kerr Country Fair, 1979. *From the* Kerrville Mountain Sun, *www. Newspapers.com.*

States governments. The band's brand of Lone Star bluegrass was well received all across Mexico.

The band would play its last shows in 1984.

EARL GARNER AND THE BLUEGRASS MOUNTAINEERS

I started getting really interested in the banjo in 1975 at the age of thirteen. I remember seeing a band in Glen Rose, Texas, called Earl Garner and the Bluegrass Mountaineers, and the sound they had still rings in my mind, especially Earl on fiddle and R.L. Johnson on banjo. They had a great drive that I still love to hear. My Grandpa Self played fiddle and had regular jam sessions with a country/bluegrass band he played in. The guitar player also played banjo, and he would let me play around on it. I fell in love with it.
—Scott Vestal[76]

East Texas fiddler Earl Garner met fellow Texan and banjo player R.L. Johnson at an Oklahoma bluegrass festival in 1969. The two would soon form a band, Earl Garner and the Bluegrass Mountaineers.

Soon, the band would find itself recording for Stoneway Records, a bluegrass and country label based in Houston, Texas. "We recorded enough for two albums in that one session, 'cause it was all stuff we were playing all the time, so we didn't have no rehearsing or anything."[77]

In 1971, Stoneway released *Cuttin' Bluegrass*, and in 1972, it released *Texas Bluegrass*. In 1972, Stoneway would also release an Earl Garner solo album,

Earl Garner grand champion at fiddle contest in Kaufman

Earl Garner won the grand championship at the fiddle contest in Kaufman this past weekend. Two people from Paris placed in the contest.

Ted Hasten of Paris attended the contest and brought back the results for Sallie Goodin.

70-And-Over Age Division: 1st — Roy Mattox, 2nd — C. D. Hughes, 3rd — Oren Weeks.

41-69 Age Division: 1st — Earl Garner, 2nd — T. G. Hasten of Paris, 3rd — J. T. Bryan of Paris.

Youth Division: 1st — Brent Fralicks, 2nd — Connie Roberts.

Guitar Contest: Clint Welch.

musical; Southeast Chapter of the Sooner Fiddlers Association, Senior Citizens Center.

July 12 — Lampasas, Texas, Lampasas Spring Ho Festival Fiddlers Contest, 1 p.m., Hancock Park, Highway 218 South, TOTFA

July 17-18 — Falls of the Rough, Ky., The Official Kentucky State Old Time Fiddlers Championships, Rough River Dam State Resort Park, Ky. Hwy. 79 between Leitchfield and Hardinsburg.

July 24 — Hugo, Okla., Monthly musical, Red River Chapter of the Sooner Fiddlers Association; 13th Place Community Center (Housing Authority).

Aug. 5-8 — Galax, Va., 52nd Annual Old Fiddlers' Convention, Felts Park, 703 236-6355

Aug. 8 — Oxford, Ala., Alabama State Fiddle Championship, 205-238-8336.

Above: Earl Garner, grand champion fiddler. *From* Paris News, *July 9, 1987.*

Right: A 1972 advertisement for Earl Garner and the Bluegrass Mountaineers. *From the* Denton Record Chronicle, *April 20, 1972.*

Bluegrass Musical

April 22, 1972
8:00 to 11:00 P.M.

Featuring Earl Garner and the Bluegrass Mountaineers, the Watkins Family of Shreveport, La., and the Village Creek Ramblers from the Fort Worth area.

Oakdale Park

Glen Rose, Texas
Adm.: $1.00 for adults
Children 12 & under Free

This is a preview of the Bluegrass Festival to be held May 26th. to 28th.

Bluegrass Fiddler. The band would also release a 45-rpm single, "When the Angels Come for Me."

Though he was a highly proficient fiddler, playing music did not pay the bills. Garner worked for many years as a maintenance supervisor for the Texas Department of Criminal Justice Department and as a welder. Garner would record one more album in his career. *Crossing Crooked Creek* was performed with his wife and former Bluegrass Mountaineer, Frances Garner. However, Garner would stay involved in music by competing in (and winning) fiddle contests.

Some of his wins included the Senior division at the 1985 Bloomburg, Texas Fiddle Contest; grand champion at the 1987 Kauffman, Texas Fiddle Contest; and grand champion at the 1987 Quitman, Texas Fiddle Contest.

In 2002, Garner played fiddle on the album *Come and Dine* by Rod Moag and Texas Grass. In 2008, Garner won the senior division (over sixty) at the twentieth annual Branson (Missouri) Olde Time Fiddle Festival.[78] Earl Garner passed on August 14, 2013.

GERALD JONES

Gerald Jones is a phenomenal musician. I remember him from when I lived in Arlington, Texas, in the '70s. He was always the guy willing to show you how he played those cool licks in jam sessions. I learned a lot from him and am thankful that I got to meet him early on. He is also the guy that invented the Jones banjo pickup, which I have several of and have used them for years. He's very innovative.
—Scott Vestal [79]

Gerald Jones was born in the town of Gainesville, Texas, about seventy miles north of Dallas. Jones was exposed to music from an early age. His father, Elbert, was a musician who played in various dance bands. It wasn't until his teen years that Gerald became inspired to pick up the guitar, after hearing singer/songwriter James Taylor.

Shortly after that, Gerald discovered the instrument that he would ultimately devote the most time to while watching the *Glen Campbell Show*. After seeing John Hartford play the banjo, he became fascinated with it. His parents gave him a student banjo as a high school graduation present. Jones spent countless hours with the instrument, which he described to Wilbur Whitten of *Banjo Newsletter* in 2004:

> *I got so into banjo and I played it so much that my fingernails grew flat underneath on my first two fingers. I had these permanent marks on my first two fingers. I'd have picks on my hands seven, eight, nine hours a day.* [80]

As he was becoming more familiar with the banjo, Gerald became acquainted with Robert Davis, a friend of his father, Elbert, who was also a musician. Davis took Gerald to his first bluegrass festival and also to rehearsals with his band:

> *At that time, Robert was playing in a group called the Stone Mountain Boys, who were regionally well known. Byron Berline was in the band at one time—Alan Munde and different folks. The banjo player in that [group] was Eddie Shelton, who is probably my first big influence. Eddie was local, and I would go with Robert to their rehearsals. I didn't know that they were a real good bluegrass band—I thought everybody was that good.* [81]

Gerald Jones in Driftwood, Texas, 2016. *Photograph courtesy of Rick Gardner.*

Gerald continued to progress in his abilities as a banjoist. Although he did not receive formal instruction on the instrument, he would pick up tips from other players at various festivals and jam sessions. Jones was also performing with various local bands. One of these groups consisted of students attending the University of North Texas in Denton. They eventually became known as Roanoke and would go on to record one album on Slim Richey's Ridge Runner label. Jones also started doing work as a studio musician around this time. He recorded with various artists, such as Dan Huckabee, Country Gazette, Sam Bush and Mark O'Connor.

After leaving Roanoke, Gerald moved to Louisville, Kentucky. While there, he was the banjoist for a short-lived group called Lazy River. The group's lead singer and guitarist was Country Hall of Fame member Vince Gill. After Lazy River disbanded, Jones moved back to the Dallas area, where he did freelance work with numerous artists.[82]

Gerald also had knowledge in electronics, which he was able to utilize when he invented the Jones Acoustic Plus, an electric pickup specifically designed for acoustic banjos. This system was utilized by many renowned banjoists, such as Earl Scruggs and Bela Fleck.[83]

Throughout his career, Gerald has performed with various groups, such as Acoustic Plus, featuring Texas Shorty (Jim Chancellor) on fiddle and Jones's wife, Leigh Taylor. Beginning in the 2010s, Gerald contributed his abilities on banjo and mandolin to Sgt. Pepper's Lonely Bluegrass Band, a four-piece band that specializes in acoustic renditions of songs by the Beatles.

Along with performing and recording, Gerald also specialized in teaching up-and-coming musicians. He has taught private lessons in banjo, mandolin, guitar and fiddle and has also released instructional materials for Mel Bay. Over the years, he has also conducted banjo workshops at various music camps and festivals around the United States. He eventually founded the Acoustic Music Camp in Arlington, Texas.

KARL SHIFLETT

In 1968, an eleven-year-old boy attended the first Old Time Fiddlers Convention in Groesbeck, Texas. Groesbeck is one hundred miles south of Dallas and sixteen miles from Kosse, the birthplace of Bob Wills. For this eleven-year-old boy, the convention would strike a chord that would change his life. Although there were guitar players in his family, the fusion of banjos, guitars and fiddles resonated deeply with young Karl Shiflett.

> *I first heard bluegrass music up close and in person at the first annual fiddlers contest held in my hometown, Groesbeck, Texas, in the mid '60s. This was the days before bluegrass festivals had started, and pickers who played bluegrass would gather at old-time fiddlers' contests to jam with one another under the trees. While the primary focus was on Texas-style fiddling, the event brought in musicians from all over, so there was a good representation of various styles of acoustic country music. I really loved the fiddle music, but I was drawn to the shade trees, where the bluegrass music was being played. Bottom line is that this was a life-changing encounter, and at the end of the day, I went home with a desire and determination to learn to play music.*[84]

Karl's great-grandfather had fashioned an instrument out of a cigar box during the Great Depression. Karl used this as a template to build his first fiddle. The local barber played fiddle, and Karl would hang out at the barbershop for the Saturday afternoon jams.

Realizing there was hot fiddler in town, Karl switched to guitar. "I spent the next year trying to learn fiddle. By the time the next year came around, I could play a rough version of a couple of tunes. I soon realized I might be able to participate in the jams a little more if I played guitar. From that point

Karl Shiflett. *Photograph courtesy of Michael G. Stewart.*

on, I started focusing on bluegrass music."[85] Joining in on the jams is where he learned to sing and play guitar. "Old-time fiddling, bluegrass, western swing, honky-tonk—we played it all back then. The musicians were all very kind to me and gave me encouragement. Something I never forgot."[86]

Karl's second musical epiphany happened at a high school auditorium in Corsicana, Texas. The auditorium was hosting a show by Lester Flatt and the Nashville Grass, featuring a very young Marty Stuart. The chance to see highly proficient bluegrass musicians perform influenced Karl to pursue music professionally.

In 1975, Karl started jamming with D.L. Rollins and his son Travis in Waco, Texas. D.L. owned a battery shop on Fifteenth Street in Waco. By 1976, they had formed the band Brazos Grass and soon had a weekly radio show on KMIL out of Cameron, Texas. The radio show lasted until 1978.

As a musician who is equally proficient in guitar, mandolin, banjo and bass, Karl spent the next few years playing in multiple bands across the Lone Star State. He filled in on bass with the Humbert Brothers. After he joined up with Bill Stokes's band Jackson County, named after Bill's birthplace of Jackson County, Tennessee, he also played with Southern Heritage, the Coleman Brothers and Joe Featherston and the Country Travelers. "Joe was a good guitar player and singer and great front man for a band. I learned a lot about leading a band from him."[87] He finally met the Sullivan family in 1985 and played with them on a part-time basis.

He would continue this part-time arrangement while also playing with Chubby Wise, Mac Wiseman and others, until 1991, when he joined the Sullivan family full time. "Joining the Sullivan family was my first professional traveling job."[88] Karl stayed with the Sullivan family through the end of 1992, when he struck out on his own.

The Karl Shiflett and Big Country Show would make their debut in 1993. The band would travel across the United States, entertaining audiences through the '90s and into the new millennium.

The band traveled extensively, selling their own DYI cassettes until finally recording their first album, *The Karl Shiflett & Big Country Show*, in 1999. The album featured the chart toping single, "Where the Smoke Goes Up." Over the next sixteen years, the band would release four (only three listed) more albums, *In Full Color*, *Take Me Back* and *Sho Nuff Country*.

In January 2020, the Karl Shiflett and Big Country Show rolled into their fourth decade of making music.

CENTRAL TEXAS BLUEGRASS ASSOCIATION (CTBA)

Authors' note: This article was contributed and copyrighted by Ken Brown in 2002. Ken (dobro, guitar) is a native Austinite in the PhD program at UT–Austin. Ken plays (mostly dobro) with the Blackland Prairie Boys. He says the Boys don't let him sing in public, and he has the severed microphone cords to prove it. The article covers the Central Texas Bluegrass Association from 1977 to 2002.

Even if you've noticed the "1978" in the association's logo, or if you've noticed that this issue is part of volume 25, the significance of that may have escaped you. Well, the CTBA is now twenty-five years old, presumably placing it among the oldest local and regional bluegrass associations in the country. Steve has asked me to write this retrospective essay, perhaps because I'm a relic of the past myself, and in it, I intend not only to review some of the association's history, but also to assess where we stand as an organization. We have a distinguished history of faithful support for bluegrass in Central

Central Texas Bluegrass
Association Jam at St. Elmo
Brewing Co., Austin, Texas.
Photograph courtesy of Libby Brennan.

Texas, and it won't hurt to review some past accomplishments. As I type, I'm listening to my favorite internet bluegrass DJ, Lisa Kay Howard, on www. BluegrassCountry.org, and that helps speed the task along. If you're interested in local bluegrass history, I'd also like to remind you of the comprehensive two-part history of Austin bluegrass bands published by Tom Ellis in the February–March and April–May 1988 issues of the *Bulletin*.

Late 1970s: Founding and Early History

The story actually starts seven months before the founding of the CTBA, when Austinite Don Rodgers (1933–1990) started a privately published monthly *Bluegrass Newsletter*. The first issue was published in April 1977. At that time, the chief umbrella organization for acoustic musicians was our sister association, the Austin Friends of Traditional Music (AFTM, also still going strong, by the way), which hosted an open mic at the old Rome Inn on Twenty-Ninth Street. This was the chief jamming outlet for Austin-area bluegrass pickers. Before that, the AFTM sessions had been held at the Crazy Horse Saloon (on Cameron Road). These places, along with the beloved Split Rail on South Lamar Street (now the site of a Wendy's burger joint) were the hotspots for bluegrass jamming. And believe it or not, Austin already had a bluegrass radio show *Bluegrass Breakdown* on KUT-FM, hosted by Terry Lickona, now the producer of Austin City Limits. The principal Texas bluegrass festivals were at Kerrville, McKinney, Buffalo Gap, Perrin and Glen Rose (Oakdale Park).

The first planning session for a proposed Central Texas Bluegrass Association took place on October 12, 1977. Attending were Rod and Nancy Kennedy, Bob and Joyce Barton, Ken McCormick, Ted and Carla Miller, Frank Jennings, Don Rodgers, Judy Minshew and Pete Nichols. Ted Miller was the chief sparkplug for the founding of the organization. The charter membership convention took place on January 22, 1978, at the Tumbleweed Restaurant, (now the County Line restaurant on the hill, FM 2222, west of Loop 360; see photograph). Rod Kennedy was the emcee for a crowd of 120 people (61 of whom signed up to become charter members), and seven bands performed: Backyard Bluegrass, Grassfire, Southern Select, the Poverty Playboys, the Broken String Band, Southwind and No Money Down (the band that I was in at the time). There was a general membership meeting, Ted Miller was elected chairman and a board of directors was elected (including Tom Pittman and Wayne Ross). The following month was marked by the beginning of the official CTBA jam (first and third Sundays) at St. Michael's Episcopal Church on Bee Cave Road, a jam session that was to persist at the same location for the next twelve years. Since Don Rodgers already had an existing Texas-oriented bluegrass newsletter in existence, the board of directors worked out a contractual arrangement in which Don's publication was to be distributed as a benefit of membership in the CTBA. This arrangement persisted for ten years, until the association started its own newsletter in 1987. Only a few months old, the CTBA cosponsored (along with the Kerrville Music Foundation) its first public bluegrass concerts in Kerrville (McLain Family Band, Buck White and the Down Home Folks) and at the Paramount Theater in August, where fiddler Jana Jae was the headliner and 600 people turned out. And 1978 also marked the founding of Leon Valley Bluegrass, a longtime CTBA band.

The second annual meeting of the CTBA took place on February 4, 1979, at the Alamo Roadhouse, which is now the other County Line restaurant, the one on Bull Creek. Continuing the precedent set at the first meeting, several bands performed: Lower Forty Bluegrass (from Alabama), Leon Valley Bluegrass, Blue Blazes (featuring, among others, Tim Wilson), the Poverty Playboys and No Money Down. Somewhere, I still have a cassette of part of those shows. Ed Garner was elected as the new president. At this point in the incipient history of the organization, a significant proportion of the members actually showed up at the annual meetings. I can't find any attendance figures, but I seem to recall a decent-sized crowd. The CTBA's charter still provides for an annual meeting (the last one was held on December 1, 2002), but hardly anyone shows up anymore. Of course, we don't offer free beer and pizza. What were we thinking?

On April 1, the association cosponsored (with KOKE Radio, then a country station) another concert at the Silver Dollar South with Leon Valley, the Poverty Playboys, Grassfire and Southern Select.

The 1980s: Bluegrass Boomtown

In January 1980, the *Bluegrass Newsletter* went to a bimonthly schedule, and in March, the CTBA held its third annual membership convention at the Opera House in Bastrop. The board of directors defined five goals for the association:

- Buy a sound system to be used at CTBA concerts.
- Buy a banner for a membership booth.
- Build the treasury to $2,000.
- Promote one show per quarter in small towns around Austin.
- Pay bands for playing.

The *Bluegrass Breakdown* program on KUT-FM was canceled, and Bill Monroe played the Armadillo World Headquarters (November 19, 1980); the band included Kenny Baker, Wayne Lewis, Butch Robins and Mark Hembree. I shot up an entire roll of black-and-white film and managed to get some good photographs of Bill and the Bluegrass Boys. About this time, I moved to San Antonio, and for the next eight years, my knowledge of CTBA happenings is derived mostly from the newsletter. In July 1981, Jamie MacLaggan took over as editor and publisher of the *Bluegrass Newsletter*, beginning with volume 5, number 4. The CTBA continued to promote shows at the Bastrop Opera House in the summer of 1981, and it was around this time that the CTBA's logo first appeared in print. The mandolin-shaped logo was drawn by Austin dobro picker Leonard Kasza. During the early 1980s, the events calendar began to expand somewhat, and it's clear that there were more venues supporting bluegrass and more special events in the Central Texas area. The CTBA continued to promote concerts at the Bastrop Opera House. In October 1982, Dave Marcum launched a new radio program, *Bluegrass Sunday Morning*, on KVET-AM—in effect, a forerunner of the current *Strictly Bluegrass* on KOOP-FM.

The CTBA probably achieved its high-water mark in 1984 and 1985 with the successful staging (in cooperation with the UT Bluegrass Association) of two Bluegrass Winterfests at the Performing Arts Center Concert Hall on the UT campus. The first of these, held on February 10, 1984, featured the Doc Watson Trio with Sam Bush, Hot Rize, Doyle Lawson and Quicksilver and the Fire on the Mountain Cloggers. And remarkably, 2,200 of the 3,000 seats in the auditorium were filled. On March 2, 1985, the second Winterfest was presented, with the Johnson Mountain Boys and the Whites featured.

Since I lived in San Antonio, I was not involved in any of the planning or execution of these concerts, but I can well imagine what a staggering undertaking it must have been to produce two events on this scale. All I can tell you is that both years, when I walked into the auditorium and saw the immense turnout, I was amazed. And the shows themselves were unbelievably good. This was truly the CTBA's finest hour, and the association's officers ought to be enshrined somewhere for their efforts. In many ways, the mid- and late 1980s were boom times for bluegrass in Central Texas and elsewhere. The newsletter was upgraded and expanded, there were more local events, the Kerrville Bluegrass Festival continued to bring in major talent like Hot Rize and the Whites and promoter Jane Lancaster staged a series of Nacogdoches Summer Music Festivals with acts like the Seldom Scene, Osborne Brothers, Hot Rize, Newgrass Revival, Nashville Bluegrass Band, Tony Trischka and Skyline, J.D. Crowe and the New South, Jerry Douglas, the Tony Rice Unit, the Bluegrass Cardinals and others. It seemed that almost every major act in bluegrass was there, and it was at one of these that Pete Wernick ventured out into the campground one evening and spent the night picking with a bunch of us rank amateurs. In the winter, Jane also staged indoor festivals termed "Acoustic Music Conventions." In September 1988, the final Kerrville Bluegrass Festival took place, and in October, the first Old Settlers Bluegrass Festival was held in Round Rock, sponsored by the Old Settlers Association, City of Round Rock and the Round Rock Chamber of Commerce. The following year, I saw Alison Krauss and Union Station for the first time at the second festival.

In September 1984, *Bluegrass Sunday Morning* was canceled. In May 1984, the CTBA and Ted Miller took over the publication of the *Bluegrass Newsletter* from Jamie MacLaggan, maintaining both the name and the current issue numbering of the publication (the next three issues lack the year of publication). The CTBA also established a new "north" jam at Old Settlers Park on weekends that alternated with the St. Michael's jam. In October 1986, the "north" jam moved to Cap'n Tom's Barbecue. I believe Rolf and Beate Sieker made their first visit to Austin in January 1985, and later that same year, the IBMA was chartered (in 1992, the CTBA joined as a member organization).

In 1986, the first Tres Rios Festival was held, featuring, among others, Blue Night Express. Didn't a couple of those pickers eventually become Dixie Chicks?

In 1987, the final issue of the *Bluegrass Newsletter* was published (April–May 1987, volume 11, number 2), and in May, the CTBA established the Central Texas Bluegrass Bulletin to fill the void left by the demise of the *Bluegrass Newsletter*.

This is the first publication that the association could truly call its own (and the first to actually sport the association's logo), and Jeanne DeFriese was the first editor. The first issue is undated but was evidently issued in

April 18, 2021, CTBA Board Band playing at Trash Talkin', County Line BBQ, Austin, Texas. *Photograph courtesy of Natalie Turner.*

May 1987. Eleven issues in seven-by-eight-and-a-half-inch format were produced at irregular intervals, the last being the December 1988/January 1989 issue. The date was listed beginning with the second issue, but no volume or issue numbers were listed. Beginning with the February–March 1989 issue, the *Bulletin* went back to a standard eight-and-a-half-by-eleven-inch format, very similar in appearance to the *Bluegrass Newsletter* but with the logo on the masthead. Volume and issue numbers were still omitted throughout 1989, until the February–March 1990 issue was published as volume 12, number 1. The numbering, in other words, was resumed in such a way as to make it consistent with its predecessor, the *Bluegrass Newsletter*. CTBA member Buck Buchanan handled the printing of the *Bulletin* and would continue to do so for the next ten years, earning himself a place in the CTBA Hall of Honor.

On May 7, 1988, the association celebrated its tenth anniversary and Worldwide Bluegrass Month by staging the first of eleven annual outdoor public concerts at Zilker Hillside Theater. Wrygrass, the Barnburners, the Grazmatics, Texas Prairie Fire, the Buchanan Brothers, Leon Valley Bluegrass and the Flaky Biscuit Boys played. In 1990, Don McCalister suggested that the CTBA issue a compilation recording, representing all the member bands, to raise funds for the CTBA. Now, thirteen years later, it looks as though that idea is going to assume concrete form, as the association plans to issue its first compilation CD.

The 1990s: Zilker and Old Settlers

In June 1990, the CTBA biweekly jam ended its twelve-year run at St. Michael's Church, leaving the "alternate north" jam session at Cap'n Tom's Barbecue on North Lamar Street (now Ross's Old Austin Café) as the official CTBA jam and starting a tradition of "barbecue and bluegrass" that continues in Austin to this day. Tom Allen, the North Carolinian ex–tugboat captain, served as our genial host for the next year and a half. Large measures of bluegrass were picked on the wraparound porch, and stage shows featuring acts like the Weary Hearts and Warrior River Boys were often held on a small open stage in the front yard. In about January 1993, the jam moved to the Travis County Farmers' Market on Burnet Road and, for the first time, was held every Sunday.

In October 1992, the CTBA sponsored a fall festival (with the Del McCoury Band) at Jellystone Park, near Waller. In December, John Hood became the editor of the *Bulletin*. In 1993, the association cosponsored the Old Settlers Festival. This was the only year that the CTBA was formally involved with the festival, but because so many CTBA members continued to volunteer in subsequent years and because the CTBA continued to hold its own events at Old Settlers Park, the festival was often erroneously associated with the CTBA in years to come. A show featuring Bill Monroe and the Bluegrass Boys was scheduled for June 12, 1994, at the Manchaca Fire Hall but had to be canceled. In July 1994, the CTBA jam moved from the farmers' market to Ruby's Barbecue, on Twenty-Ninth Street. *Strictly Bluegrass*, hosted by Keith Davis and Rod Moag, went on the air on KOOP-FM in 1994. In 1995, the board of directors began seeking cultural arts funding for the Zilker Show from the City of Austin. The grant was received and applied to the 1996 festival. In April 1995, the CTBA jam moved from Ruby's Barbecue to ArtZ RibHouse, where it remains today, and in July, the association began holding its annual "Fun Raiser" Garage Sale at ArtZ RibHouse to recover losses (about $500) from producing the Zilker Festival and actually took in $863, far exceeding its goal. Sometime around February 1996, the CTBA website went online. At the urging of editor John Hood and beginning with the June 1996 issue, the *Bulletin* was considerably downsized and changed from a bimonthly to a monthly publication. Chuck Interrante became the new editor in November 1996, then Chuck Brodkin in April 1997, Doug Stoker in July 1998 and the present editor, Steve Zimmet, in March 2000.

For eleven years, from 1988 to 1999, the CTBA held its free outdoor concert series at Zilker Park Hillside Theater in May, through years with good weather and bad, subsidizing it through arts funding (in the early years) and the July "Fun-Raiser." Rising use fees and declining city funding led the association to discontinue the Zilker Festival in 2000. Instead, an association jam was held at Krause Springs in May 2000, and a fall festival was held at Old Settlers Park (by this time, the "Old Settlers Festival," promoted by Randy Collier, had moved on to Dripping Springs).

Unfortunately, a cold rain kept the crowds away in droves, and the audience was estimated at about ninety for the day. A fall "Pick-Nic" for members was also held at Quarries Park in northwest Austin from 1996 to 1999. Board members began to be concerned with the decline in the association membership (see the January 2001 issue of the *Bulletin*). In March 2001, the board met for a retreat to discuss goals and strategies for the association. A monthly meeting with a featured paid band was suggested, as was seeking grants and corporate donations for funding. In October 2001, another fall festival was held at Old Settlers Park.

Festivals, Concerts and Workshops

As the preceding history reveals, the CTBA has presented an amazing array of live music during its twenty-five-year history, beginning with the nascent organization's very first annual meeting. This part of its mission statement has been well executed, with eleven years at Zilker, four years at the Quarries, several festivals at Old Settlers Park and a variety of concerts by touring bands. The two major concerts at the Performing Arts Center in the mid-1980s were the climax of this effort.

The jam session is another success story. It's never been more healthy than it is right now. Pickers can show up at ArtZ RibHouse just about any Sunday and count on finding an assortment of like-minded jam partners. Dependability and a good host are the keys to a good jam session, and we have both. We have been very fortunate in having support from gracious hosts like Tom Allen, Art Blondin and Zenobia Sutton. If you go to ArtZ to pick or listen to shows, buy something to eat. Art didn't win all those barbecue cook-off awards on the walls for nothing, you know.

In reality, the CTBA doesn't have to do anything to sponsor the jam session. ArtZ RibHouse supplies the location, and all we have to do is show up. For a time, the CTBA had a semiformal "jam coordinator" (Ron Wilbourn and, later, Eddie Collins), whose job was to encourage new pickers and to try to break the session into subclusters when the circle got too big. I think the association would do well to reinstate this position. If there's a drawback to the current jam, it's that it's usually too big. It's not unusual to see twenty or more pickers in a circle trying to play the same tune, often without even being able to see one another. Tunes take fifteen minutes to rotate around the circle. Someone needs to enforce cell division on the larger sessions.

Education and Promotion Functions

The growth of the association depends on new members, and that means reaching existing bluegrass fans who don't yet know about us, as well as making new bluegrass converts. The CTBA has been struggling toward this goal for its entire life. As I remarked earlier, this isn't really bluegrass territory. Most Central Texans are more familiar with Christina Aguilera than Mountain Heart. Even the sporadic appearance of Alison Krauss on KGSR's playlist hasn't really helped inform the public much, although I do think that radio is the best medium for reaching the public. See "Pitching Bluegrass to Commercial Radio" at www.ibma.org. Even as we speak, the IBMA is starting a new "Discover Bluegrass" marketing campaign. Ken Brown said, "Maybe we need to get involved in that."

The Central Texas Bluegrass Association reached its fortieth anniversary in 2018 and is still going strong, sponsoring events, contests and scholarships for young musicians who want to carry on the bluegrass tradition.

CTBA president Libby Brennan talks about what bluegrass means to her and the local community:

> *I have a short history with bluegrass, but it has been profound. My first bluegrass night was Monday at Flipnotics in 2011. For anyone who knows Flips, they know that the room was minimal. When the pickers started, immediately, the room turned into a sound bowl. You could hardly fit all five pickers on stage. Banjo, bass, mando, guitar, fiddle, ricocheted off the four very small walls. Immediately, I was awash. It was like a religious experience.*
>
> *From there, I met the very talented and humble crew of Wood & Wire, who, in their infancy, came over to my house one very cold February, drank some whiskey and picked for a small group of friends by the fire.*
>
> *This is grass.*
>
> *I have attended as many bluegrass nights as possible over the last decade. Single, in love, out of love, pregnant, with child. My child has a genetic disposition for toe tappin' in tune. I see the music washing through her soul.*
>
> *Bluegrass is a part of my happiness and a place that has extrapolated me from some of my darkest days. I am so grateful to be a part of this community that is so rich in talent, knowledge and the gift of community.*
>
> *Bluegrass is a place to put aside our differences, escape our heartbreak, feel the instruments and heal.*[89]

If you find yourself in the Austin, Texas area, join the CTBA at one of their many jams. The Sunday jam at Oskar Blues Brewery Austin, the bimonthly beginner/intermediate jam at Wildflower Terrace and the monthly jam at St. Elmo Brewing Company. Natalie Turner, CTBA board member and secretary, said:

> *The Austin bluegrass scene is thriving. It's grown so much over the years that you can find performances and jams almost any day of the week.*

The growing number of organizations, venues and festivals in support of bluegrass is inspiring to witness. Our community includes talented musicians of all ages, friendly music-lovers and even some of the best pickers in the country![90]

www.centraltexasbluegrass.org

Slim Richey: The Most Dangerous Guitarist in Texas

"The most dangerous guitarist in Texas"—so read the marquee at the historic Paramount Theatre in Austin on June 1, 2015, the day before the iconic, eccentric musician David Michael "Slim" Richey had passed away from lymphoma.

Slim was born on February 11, 1938, in Atlanta, Texas. Who better to tell his story than one of his longtime collaborators, banjo virtuoso Alan Munde?

I met David Michael Richey [also known as Slim Richey] in the early 1960s, when he ran a music store, Mike Richey's Guitar Center, a few blocks from my home in Norman, Oklahoma. Slim was from Atlanta, Texas. Atlanta is in far northeast corner of Texas, near the Louisiana border and under the cultural influence of Shreveport, Louisiana. He heard the country music of the area and the sounds of the Louisiana Hayride, *one of the seminal country music radio programs of the 1950s. As a budding guitarist, he was also hip to the sounds of the jazz guitar of Herb Ellis, Barney Kessel, Tal Farlow, Jimmy Raney, Charlie Christian and others.*

At the time I met Slim, he saw himself as primarily a jazz guitarist but certainly enjoyed and appreciated all the stringed instrument styles that were going in the 1960s—rock, folk, bluegrass, jazz, classical. As a seller of the guitars, banjos, mandolins and an occasional fiddle, he played a bit on each, and in different styles to demonstrate their qualities. I hung out a lot in his store, picking up all sorts of musical information and attitudes about music and life from the patrons but mostly from Slim. During my last couple of years at the University of Oklahoma, I taught guitar and banjo at his store.

Slim left town; I left town, but we kept in touch. When he returned to the area, moving to Fort Worth, Texas, I had then moved back to Norman, he approached me about recording for his then-forming label, Ridge Runner.

Sim Richey with Francie Meaux Jeaux in Houston, 1997. *Photograph courtesy of Rick Gardner.*

We did several recordings of banjo/bluegrass instrumental music that did well for both him and me. Slim also got into mail order instrument sales with Warehouse Music Sales. Additionally, he had a trailer full of instruments, records, cassettes, T-shirts, strings, picks, capos and instrument accessories of many kinds he would pull to the many burgeoning weekend bluegrass music festivals in Texas, Oklahoma, Louisiana and anywhere he felt would be profitable. In the evenings, when he closed up the trailer, he would participate in the many late-evening jam sessions.

He sensed that there were a lot of the bluegrass pickers, especially the younger set, who were also interested in expanding their musical horizons by trying some of the older jazz standards, such as "Sweet Georgia Brown," "Lady Be Good," "Back Home Again in Indiana" and others. This coupling of his interest and abilities in the jazz guitar realm, with the perceived interest of these bluegrassers in trying new—for them—musical challenges is the birth of jazz grass. He gathered the professional and adventurous players he had come to know through his sales and festival experiences (me, Joe Carr, Gerald Jones, Sam Bush,

Ricky Skaggs, Dan Huckabee) and those recommended to him (Bill Keith and Richard Greene).

He added a couple a DFW jazz players (bassist Kerby Stewart and guitarist Jerry Case). He also had a Fort Worth local record store owner and blues guitar specialist, Sumter Bruton, to play on Bruton's composition "Boppin' at the Bluebird." We recorded all the tracks at a studio in Fort Worth. Slim sent the tape of "Night in Tunisia," to Massachusetts for Bill Keith to add his banjo part. Roland White and I were recording in an LA studio for a Slim project that Richard Greene was on. Slim was in attendance and had Richard record his part on "Jazz Grass Waltz" after Roland and I were finished for the day.

I, as a bluegrass banjo player, had few models to follow. Allen Shelton, Eddie Adcock, Don Reno, Walter Hensley and Roger Sprung had recorded pop tunes on the banjo, all in a bluegrass context, which is one way to do it. Slim wanted to move further into the jazz sensibility of rhythm and harmony and soloing. I don't believe I played the head on any of the tunes, only "improvised" solos. I tried my best but feel that my efforts had an awkward result. I did like my solo on "There"l Never Be Another You." I also like the opening riff and my solo on "Jazz Grass Waltz." The other banjoists, Gerald Jones and Bill Keith, were more successful than I. Gerald, on banjo, and Joe, on mandolin, played, in unison, their copy of a Charlie Christian solo for "Stopping at the Savoy," which I thought was very cool. Bill Keith recorded a wonderful rendition of "Night in Tunisia."

Over the years, I think our efforts have stood up well, although I do remember one reviewer at the time commenting that it didn't sound like any of the Dave Brubeck records he owned. Slim could only agree.[91]

Aside from the jazz grass album, Ridge Runner Records issued albums from many prominent artists. Marty Stuart's first album, *With a Little Help from My Friends*, was issued by Ridge Runner in 1978. Other artists who issued albums from Ridge Runner included Alison Brown, Stuart Duncan, Sam Bush, Kenny Baker, Muleskinner, Roanoke, Eddie Shelton, Wayne Stewart, the Stone Mountain Boys, the Tennessee Gentlemen, Buck White, Joe Carr and Roland White.

Slim played guitar on 1979's Country Gazette album, *All This and Money Too*. Then, in 1981, Slim produced and played guitar on the Country Gazette album *American & Clean*, released by Flying Fish Records.

Slim also played for a short while with Salt Lick Foundation. Salt Lick was a Dallas-Fort Worth–area bluegrass-centric bar band. Salt Lick Foundation was formed in the mid-1970s, and they did not take themselves too seriously. This was obvious, as their signature song was a bluegrass cover of Jimi Hendrix's "Are You Experienced?" Salt Lick was also a frequent guest on the *Dr. Demento Show* (1970–2010), a syndicated radio show created by Barret Eugene "Barry" Hansen. The show had an all-novelty format specializing in offbeat, strange comedy songs. Before breaking up, the band would record three albums: *Rural Lust & Urban Rust* (1980), *Daynce of the Peckerwoods* (1982) and *Salt Lick Sockeroos* (1985).

Richey would relocate to Driftwood, Texas, in 1992 and perform throughout the Hill Country for the next two decades. Slim would also become a mentor to young musicians and a fixture at the Kerrville Folk and Old Settlers Music Festivals.

Slim was a performer at Fort Worth's Django Reinhardt Festival with his band, Slim Richey's Stray Gypsies. Slim was a huge Django Reinhardt fan. The Fort Worth festival is sponsored by Arts Fifth Avenue. Art Fifth Avenue founder and artistic director Gracey Tune said of Slim, "He helped me start the Django Festival eighteen years ago."[92] Alan Munde tells the story of how western swing bands would loan Slim Django records at his Oklahoma music store. The Django records were hard-to-find items in those days.[93]

On May 20, 2015, eleven days before Slim Richey passed away, Texas mandolinist Nate Lee recorded Slim's song "Jazz Grass Waltz" for his album *Plays Well with Others*. Nate stated that the song was a favorite among the bluegrass students during his time at South Plains College. Slim Richey: still expanding musical horizons.

HICKORY HILL

In 1979, a small cable sports channel debuted called ESPN. The Iran Hostage Crisis started its 444-day ordeal on November 4, 1979. On December 11, music fans were crushed in a stampede for seats at a Who concert in Cincinnati, Ohio. Also in 1979, the first annual Gettysburg Bluegrass Festival was held, and Lester Flatt died at the age of sixty-four. Meanwhile, a Texas bluegrass band made a stunning debut at Rod Kennedy's Kerrville Bluegrass Festival.

Hickory Hill was the former name of Avinger, Texas, a small town in East Texas. A group of musicians from Avinger chose the name for their new band. John Early and Rolan Foster grew up together in Avinger, playing music. At college, the two best friends met saxophone player

Hickory Hill, July 4, 1986, Nacogdoches Bluegrass Festival. *Left to right*: Ronny Singley, Rolan Foster, John Early, Bob Stegall, Don Eaves. *Photograph courtesy of Rick Gardner.*

Ronny Singley, who gave up the saxophone and took up the mandolin to play with Early and Foster.

The three musicians formed the band Pecos and started playing rock and country music. Then came their musical epiphany: the band came across the music of Bill Monroe, Lester Flatt and Earl Scruggs, changing their musical direction. With Don Eaves joining the band on banjo and Bob Stegall on bass, Hickory Hill took the bluegrass world by storm at the 1979 Kerrville Bluegrass Festival. Don Rodgers said:

> *Among the many good things to come out of Rod Kennedy's Kerrville Festival's is Hickory Hill. It was at the 1979 Bluegrass Festival that the group came together as a full-fledged bluegrass band. On that occasion, Rolan Foster, Ronny Singley, John Early and Bob Stegall (all from around Tyler in East Texas) met Don Eaves, a banjo player form their own area. That, plus lots of hard work, was all these talented and experienced musicians needed to become (in less than two years) one of the hottest new bands in bluegrass.*[94]

After their stunning debut in Kerrville, numerous accolades followed, such as:

- Winning third place in the "Best New Band" contest at the 1981 Bluegrass Festival of the United States in Louisville, Kentucky.
- The 1985 nomination for "Entertaining Bluegrass Band of the Year" from the Society for the Preservation of Bluegrass Music of America.
- The 1986 nomination for "Bluegrass Band of the Year, Contemporary" from the Society for the Preservation of Bluegrass Music of America.
- Being the host band of the Overton Bluegrass Music Festival from the festival's inception in 1989.
- Being named 1993's "Band of the Year" by the Arts and Entertainment Committee of East Texas.

From 1982 to 1990, Hickory Hill released four albums: *Coyote Night* (1982), *Special Historical Edition* (1983), *It's About Time* (1985) and *Reminiscin'* (1990). All four of the albums were enthusiastically embraced by bluegrass fans, and all four received positive critical reviews. In reviewing *It's About Time*, Ted Miller of the *Bluegrass Newsletter* said, "If all the albums produced sounded like this, bluegrass would be at the top of the record charts."[95]

In 1994, the Turquoise Records label out of Whitesburg, Kentucky, signed the band to a new contract. The first release from Turquoise Records was a compilation of their first four albums. The new album was well received across the country and north of the border in Canada. A Canadian bluegrass reviewer described *The First Fifteen Years* as "chock full of creative lyrics and instrumental high points." A review of the album in *Dirty Linen* said, "Hickory Hill is a cross between poco gone grass and a dirt band that bathes with a splash of Bill Monroe."[96]

In 1996, Hickory Hill was selected for a showcase performance at the International Bluegrass Music Association's annual World of Bluegrass in Owensboro, Kentucky. However, 1996 would bring tragedy as well triumph for the band, as Rolan Foster passed away from cancer. Just as Dickey Betts stepped up to fill a void in the Allman Brothers after Duane Allman passed, John Early had a to fill the space left by the death of his childhood friend and musical companion.

Jimmy Godwin, who had played in the old Pecos band joined Hickory Hill in 1997. In 1998, the band released its fifth album *Good Times Again*. Heading

Hickory Hill's album *Coyote Night*. *Photograph courtesy of Jeff Campbell.*

into the new millennium, Hickory Hill released its first gospel album, *Thank You Lord*. Not long after the album's release, the band experienced its second loss with the death of Jimmy Godwin.

In 2002, the band looked forward to recording its eighth album, *Freedom*. But prior to the sessions, Ronny Singley decided to hang up his mandolin and retire from the road. In his place, two mandolin players, West Texan Wes Perry and an old friend named Mike Tucker added their talents to the new album. Another compadre of Hickory Hill, Milo Deering, added fiddle and dobro to the album. *Freedom* was released in the summer of 2002, and Wes Perry joined the band as a full-time member. In 2006, Hickory Hill followed up *Freedom* with *Old School*. The latest offering was a traditional bluegrass project.

In 2009, Don Eaves decided to retire from performing. It's tough to replace a guy that can sing and play guitar and banjo. Wes Perry filled in admirably, going back and forth between banjo and mandolin until Jake Jenkins came along. Jake was a veteran of *The Karl Shifflett and Big Country Show* and joined Hickory Hill as a vocalist, guitarist and banjo player. However, only a year and half later, Jake was killed in a plane accident at the young age of forty.

The tragedy of Jake's untimely passing placed Wes Perry back into his role of alternating between mandolin and banjo.

In 2017, the Hickory Hill lineup consisted of John Early on guitar, Bob Stegall on bass, Don Eaves on banjo and guitar, Ronny Singley on mandolin, Milo Deering on fiddle and dobro and Richard Bowden on his B-Bender guitar. To celebrate its fortieth anniversary, the band released a new album, *Forty Years and Counting…*, in 2019.

The band has held an annual Winter Bluegrass Show at Music City Texas, located in Linden, Texas. In 2020, the opening band for the show was the Purple Hulls. Don Eaves taught the Purple Hulls, sisters Penny Lea Clark and Katy Clark, how to play the banjo when they were seventeen. The Texas bluegrass torch is being passed on to the next generation.

DANNY BARNES

Banjoist Danny Barnes has collaborated with Dave Matthews, Bill Frisell, Chuck Leavell and Robert Earl Keene, among others. However, mainstream bluegrass listeners have probably never heard of him. Danny Barnes was born in December 1961 in Temple, Texas, grew up in Belton and graduated from the University of Texas in 1985. Growing up in Texas is not exactly part of the bluegrass banjo's footprint of influence. What influenced his initial interest and cultivated his musical growth?

> *My mother's family was from Tennessee; my father's family was from Alabama, and as such, they were huge* Opry *fans. Also, in the sixties and seventies, they used to have musicians on TV, and there were only three channels. In the pre-postmodern milieu, media showed musicians. So, one could see various banjo playing and fiddling on the TV without too much effort. My parents were of the ilk that country music was like a laymen's Bible or something. The music was venerated and so forth.* [97]

Danny Barnes. *Photograph courtesy of Danny Barnes.*

In 1990, Danny formed the Bad Livers, an Austin band that played a combination of bluegrass, folk, punk, blues and polka. From 1991 to 2000, the band released seven albums, a soundtrack and an EP. Like other critically claimed underground bands, such as Jason and the Scorchers or Blue Mountain, were the Bad Livers ahead of their time or did they make their own lane?

I can't really comment on that, lacking the perspective of how one is perceived, as the bard says. There certainly weren't any bands like we had at the time. And there were a whole lot of our ideas that later made a lot of other people a lot of money. Maybe we were; I'm not sure. We came from the impetus that one should challenge the audience and shoot over their heads and slightly confuse them all the time. I guess that's more from the modernist like Bill Monroe and Miles Davis and so forth. Not to compare us to them, of course, but being inspired by those type people. In the postmodern world or whatever this is, (we started noticing it about the time they started having music conferences; the first SXXW was in the mid-/late '80s there—that's when a giant arm of the industry was born that made money off all the other stuff), artists try to only *do what the hypothetical audience wants. The last thing they want to do is confuse anybody. It's like looking at baseball before they had steroids. It vaguely resembles it, but it's a different animal.*[98]

Initially, the Bad Livers were not embraced by the Austin music scene. Most likely, this was due to the inability to slot them into a specific genre.

I don't know if it's possible to say that Austin is or was an inclusive welcoming community in that sense. Were there cool people and cool bands and cool venues? Yes!

But a community seeks to reward those that adhere to certain definitions or signposts. It's all well and good if you are at the top of some hierarchy and so forth. But alas, we were not. We had no drums. We didn't have a guitarist. We wore street clothes. We made fun of the audience. We played a difficult-to-define music that was a mashup up of lots of divergent things. In a moment when we had a bunch of media attention, we delivered a home-recorded gospel cassette that confused the crap out of everybody. We changed our name and played off nights, so no one would come except the dearest fans who were in on the secret. We just liked playing; it wasn't all a total money grab.

See, there was nothing really for anyone that is muckity-muck in a music community to grab onto if you do those things. But once we were in Rolling Stone *and so forth and the* New York Times *and whatnot, the British press, they accepted us a little more. And eventually, we were locally embraced beyond the fanship that we won by working super hard.*

Which is all fine. None of that stuff matters you just do it; you make stuff and do shows to finance making more stuff, and you don't have a plan B. It's all very simple.[99]

Austin would come around to the unique band with the unique sound. The Austin Music Awards voted Barnes "Best Player of Any Other Instrument" in both 1991 and 1992, and the Bad Livers was voted "Best None of the Above" from 1991 to 1994.

In the late 1990s, Danny Barnes relocated to Port Hadlock, Washington, and soon, the Bad Livers were a thing of the past. Barnes would go on to prodigious career of creativity and collaboration.

As a virtuoso musician who has never been in the bluegrass mainstream, does he think there is a traditional–progressive divide?

I don't think this is the case. That is a point usually made by someone that discovers bluegrass, perhaps not one that has kinda' of been into it since they was kids, hearing it from their folks and seeing the masters multiple times et cetera. People play different things in different periods. You like it, you don't like it. What's to get heated about? No zealot like a convert and whatnot. [100]

Also, when is bluegrass no longer bluegrass—or does it matter?

We have been stripped of meaning on so much via advertising, and that giant mechanism that sells everything I suppose. I don't know; I think bluegrass is a certain "feel." If you go back, everybody had that feel. As you move forward, the feel gets less and less, and now, nobody has that feel. That feel appears to be related to how people of the Earth have a connection to the Earth. Real working-class regular folk in small towns and stuff perhaps have a connection to the Earth and to the Bible and tradition and those sorts of aesthetics. The music is specifically designed to be a balm to the storms of life. The typical expression of it today is more from the idea of, "How clever can I be? Look at my cleverness." They have great bands; I'm not saying that. I'm more talking about the acoustic world in general of which bluegrass is a slice. If you get your hands dirty, and you actually touch the Earth and sweat and stuff, and work you get in touch with the ancient vibration; if you grow up privileged and homeschooled, and you have what's called a posh life, there is no way for one's music to have that feel. Thus, the idolatry of technique over meaning.

In 2015, Barnes received the Steve Martin Prize for excellence in banjo and bluegrass, an award that had previously been given to Noam Pikelny, Sammy Shelor and Mark Johnson.

I was completely shocked. It always amazes me that anybody listens to any of my work. I've never had the kind of success that would make the award itself look good by being bestowed on me, you dig? So, it was a total blessing and really cool of those folks. Most of the players on the board I've been listening to my entire life, so it meant a lot *to me. I come from a little tiny town in Texas.* [101]

Danny Barnes has also been a major influence on other musicians, such as Wood & Wire mandolin player, Billy Bright. He said:

For me, eventually getting to work with Danny must be what it was like for some people to get to work with Monroe. Danny is the first banjo player I ever saw live, and his group, the Bad Livers, was my first love when it came to seeing live string band music. As a human, Danny has inspired me in so many ways. I learned from him that most of the things I think I can't do, I can.[102]

In 2020, Barnes was nominated for a Grammy Award in the bluegrass album of the year category for his album, *Man on Fire*. The album has, perhaps, the most interesting supporting cast of any bluegrass album in recent history. Along with Barnes on banjo and guitar, he is joined by John Paul Jones on bass and mandolin, Matt Chamberlain on percussion, Bill Frisell on guitar and Geoff Stanfield on electric bass and piano. Dave Matthews, who produced this project, is also featured on organ and handles some vocal duties as well.

It's an album that continues Barnes's travels across the musical spectrum.

LYNN MORRIS AND MARSHALL WILBORN

Lamesa and Austin, Texas, are just hours apart from each other. In both of these towns, two different people were playing and listening to different styles of music. They would not only discover bluegrass, but they would eventually meet, start a life together and form one of the most celebrated bands within the genre.

Lynn Morris grew up in the small West Texas farming community of Lamesa.[103] Musically speaking, her first love was the guitar, which she began playing at the age of twelve. After graduating from high school, she attended Colorado College in Colorado Springs, majoring in art. During her time there, she continued playing the guitar, specifically studying jazz music with guitarist Johnny Smith.[104] Ultimately, Morris discovered the musical style that changed the trajectory of her life. While in Colorado Springs, she attended a performance by the Twenty String Bluegrass Band. Lynn found herself drawn to the sound of the banjo and just had to learn how to play it. She began studying the instrument within the next year. After graduating from college, she, along with Mary Stribling, formed the City Limits Bluegrass Band. This group performed from 1972 to 1978 and released two albums on Biscuit City Records.[105] In 1974, she won the National Banjo Championship in Winfield, Kansas. She would earn the

The Lynn Morris Band. *From left to right*: Tad Marks, Jesse Brock, Marshall Wilborn, Lynn Morris and Chris Jones. *From the author's collection.*

title again in 1981, becoming the first person to ever win twice.[106] After City Limits was dissolved, Lynn went on to perform with different country bands on USO tours, one of which included guitarist Junior Brown. In 1981, she was the guitarist for the Cherokee Rose Band.

Marshall Wilborn was born and raised in the town of Austin. He, too, would come to fall in love with the banjo. His first exposure to the instrument was through the Kingston Trio in the early 1960s. Pretty soon, an iconic instrumental piece by the famed banjoist Earl Scruggs would ultimately cement his love for bluegrass music. "I would say 'Foggy Mountain Breakdown' was the single tune that drew me into bluegrass to a point of no return. So, really, for me, it all boiled down to Flatt and Scruggs."[107] Wilborn found himself on his own as he was learning to play, as there were no other bluegrass musicians in the area. "I didn't know anybody else that had even the most remote interest in that kind of music at all. I didn't know anybody, so I just played my banjo around the house by myself."[108] It wasn't until 1971 that Marshall started meeting other like-minded musicians and jamming with them informally. Eventually, he took up the upright bass, which became his primary instrument.

In March 1982, Lynn Morris's and Marshall Wilborn's paths crossed. Wilborn recounted their first meeting:

> *Lynn was visiting her sister in San Antonio, and she called Dan Huckabee in Austin and asked Dan was there any bluegrass in Austin that she could come and check out while she was close by in San Antonio. And Dan said, "Well, as a matter of fact, I host this open mic jam at this club in downtown Austin. Why don't you come up and join us for that tomorrow evening?" So, Lynn said, "I'll be there." And then Dan immediately*

called me and said, "Lynn Morris is coming to the open mic tomorrow night, why don't you come down?"[109]

At the time, Lynn didn't know Marshall, but he was well aware of her, as he had seen her compete in Winfield, Kansas, in 1976 and also saw her at a bluegrass festival in Oklahoma just a year later.

Not long before they met, Morris had accepted an offer to join the Pennsylvania-based band Whestone Run. She moved to that area a week or two after that open mic jam in Austin. She and Wilborn kept in touch. Just a few months later, the group's bassist left, and Lynn suggested that Marshall fill the vacancy. He would ultimately join the group, but Wilborn soon realized he needed to further his musical aptitude. Lynn encouraged Marshall to go to the campus of Penn State to find someone in the music department he could take bass lessons from. "I found this grad student that was enthusiastic about showing me some stuff, and as it turns out, that's just exactly what I needed to do at the time, so I was, indeed, able to make some progress with my playing because of that."[110]

Lynn and Marshall both performed with Whetsone Run for the next four years. Following their departure from the group in 1986, Marshall served a brief stint as Jimmy Martin's bassist. Shortly after that, he received a call to join the Johnson Mountain Boys, which prompted Wilborn and Morris to relocate to Winchester, Virginia.

One of the challenges Lynn faced after the couple's relocation was finding a band that was open to hiring a female musician. Driven by this obstacle, Morris decided to form her own band in 1988. By this time, the Johnson Mountain Boys had disbanded, so Marshall partnered with Lynn in this new venture and became the group's bassist. On top of leading musically, Morris handled all of the band's business aspects, such as booking and marketing, in their early years.

Two monumental events happened for the couple and the band. In 1989, Marshall and Lynn became husband and wife. Also, at that time, Ken Irwin of Rounder Records expressed interest in potentially having the Lynn Morris Band on the label's roster. "Tom Adams and I had just come from the Johnson Mountain Boys, so we had gotten acquainted with Ken Irwin at Rounder. He was interested in our new band, but he would not commit until we had a finished product in hand to let him listen to, so when we had stuff recorded and sent to him, he was interested."[111] The recording Irwin heard was subsequently released as the band's debut album on Rounder Records in 1990.

The Lynn Morris Band went on to record four more albums, tour internationally and perform at prestigious venues, such as the Grand Ole Opry. Lynn herself received several accolades from the IBMA, such as being named female vocalist of the year in 1996, 1998 and 1999, as well as winning song of the year for her recording of "Mama's Hand," which held the number-one spot on the National Bluegrass Survey for six months after its release in 1996.[112] Morris also became the first woman ever elected to the IBMA's board of directors. She also received the "Traditional Female Vocalist" award from the SPBGMA association seven years in a row.[113]

Just two weeks after the release of the band's fifth album, *Shape of a Tear*, in 2003, Lynn Morris suffered a stroke following knee surgery. Even as she began her long recuperation, Morris wanted Marshall and the rest of the band to fulfill the performances that had been booked for that season. Wilborn ultimately found other singers to substitute for her during that period. Even though Lynn made a remarkable recovery, hand weakness and speech limitations prevented her from resuming her performance career. The Lynn Morris Band performed their final show in Vermont in 2005.[114]

Despite the Lynn Morris Band coming to an end, Lynn and Marshall remained part of the professional bluegrass music community. After a few years away, Morris returned to the road for several years as the sound engineer for Bill Emerson and Sweet Dixie.[115] In 2010, Lynn received the Distinguished Achievement Award from the IBMA.[116] In 2013, Lynn received the Washington Monument Award from the D.C. Bluegrass Union.[117] Marshall Wilborn resumed his performance career in 2007 as bassist for Michael Cleveland and Flamekeeper, with whom he would remain for the next four years.[118] From 2009 to 2012, Wilborn was named "Bass Player of the Year" by the IBMA.[119] In 2019, Marshall joined Chris Jones and the Night Drivers.

5

DID YOU KNOW?

Steve Martin

Almost everyone is aware of the comedic talents of Steve Martin. Did you know Steve Martin was a native Texan, born in Waco, Texas? Martin is also a bluegrass aficionado and a proficient picker on the banjo.

Steve Martin was born in Waco, Texas, on August 14, 1945. When Steve was five years old, his parents, Glenn Vernon Martin and Mary Lee Stewart, decided to move to Garden Grove, California. His father was an aspiring actor and felt California would provide more opportunities than Waco, Texas. However, as we all know, California would make Steve a star, not his father.

Steve started playing banjo at the age of seventeen. John McEuen of Nitty Gritty Dirt Band fame was one of Steve's early banjo teachers. The banjo became a major prop of Steve's stand-up comedy act during the 1970s.

After twenty-five years of stardom in movies and on television, Steve began to focus more on his writing and music. Martin would author books, plays, a musical and, in 2001, play banjo on Earl Scruggs's rerecording of "Foggy Mountain Breakdown."

Though Martin had released comedy albums before, in 2009, he released his first album that was totally comprised of serious music. The album was called *The Crow: New Songs for the 5-String Banjo* and features guest appearances by Tim O'Brien, Earl Scruggs, Pete Wernick, Dolly Parton, Tony Trischka and Jerry Douglas.

In 2011, Martin began a collaboration with the Steep Canyon Rangers, releasing the album *Rare Bird Alert*. Paul McCartney and the Dixie Chicks (now known as the Chicks) made guest appearances on the album. Martin

STEVE MARTIN during recent "Tonight Show" appearance

Steve Martin on the *Tonight Show* in 1977. *From the* San Antonio Express, *www.Newspapers.com.*

collaborated with the Steep Canyon Rangers on two more albums: *"Live" with Edie Brickell* (2014) and *The Long-Awaited Album* (2017).

Martin's love for bluegrass and the banjo resulted in him establishing the Steve Martin Prize for Excellence in Banjo and Bluegrass. The award has become a who's who of banjo mastery. Winners of the award have included Noam Pikelny, Danny Barnes, Rhiannon Giddens, Scott Vestal and Kristin Scott Benson.

Steve Martin has been able to use his fame to bring attention to two of his passions: the banjo and bluegrass music.

6

HONORARY TEXANS

lan Munde and Peter Rowan are two of the legendary figures in bluegrass music. Alan was born in Norman, Oklahoma, and Peter was born in Wayland, Massachusetts. However, they both spent a significant portion of their professional careers in the Lone Star State.

Alan Munde became a full-time instructor at the South Plains College's (Levelland, Texas) bluegrass and country music program in 1986. He retired from the college in 2007 and moved to Wimberley, Texas.

Peter Rowan, for many years, had been fascinated by Texas's culture and moved to Blanco, Texas, in 1990. Rowan lived in Texas for twenty-five years and collaborated with a multitude of Texas musicians from different genres.

Munde and Rowan's time in Texas is an important piece of the Texas bluegrass story.

ALAN MUNDE

Alan Munde's banjo has taken him from Norman, Oklahoma, to Dallas, Nashville, Southern California, Europe, West Texas and Wimberly, Texas.

In the late 1950s, the folk scene reached every nook and corner of the country, including Norman, Oklahoma. Young Alan Munde watched everything on television and started his musical journey on guitar. Then, one day, a banjo showed up and changed everything. The first chance he got, Alan acquired Pete Seeger's banjo book—before even owning a banjo.

Alan Munde at the 1975 Kerrville (Texas) Bluegrass Festival. *Photograph courtesy of Rick Gardner*.

Seeger played a variation on the old clawhammer technique. Alan worked out the book's basic strum on his school desk.

Then, for Christmas, a friend gave Alan a copy of Flatt and Scruggs's *Foggy Mountain Banjo* album, and the banjo fever fully took over. Alan's first banjo was a cheap Vega Ranger, purchased at Mike "Slim" Ritchie's music shop in Norman, Oklahoma. Slim introduced Alan to Gary Price from Oklahoma City. Alan took a couple of lessons from Price and then started learning on his own.

After enrolling at the University of Oklahoma, Alan met fiddle virtuoso Byron Berline. Berline would introduce Alan to Ed Shelton, who became Alan's mentor. Ed, from Texas, was stationed in Oklahoma City and was a repairman for Dayton Office Machines.

Munde would take the bus to Dallas, and musicians would pick him up for weekend jam sessions. Ed Shelton introduced Alan to some of the top players in Dallas: Mitchell Land (mandolin), Louis "Bosco" Land (guitar) and Harless "Tootie" Williams (bass). The four of them formed a band the Stone Mountain Boys in 1965. The name, Stone Mountain Boys was picked just because it sounded cool.

Byron Berline talked about the Stone Mountain Boys' influence on his musicianship:

Of course, the Stone Mountain Boys influenced my playing, as I was just getting into bluegrass music back in those days. Learning Monroe and Flatt and Scruggs and you name it. They were up on the music and studied it. They helped me a lot. I was introduced to the Stone Mountain Boys through Ed Shelton, I think. Probably around 1965, I met Tootie Williams and Mitchell Land. I had invited the boys to come and play with me on a family day basic training show; that was a lifesaving moment for me, I think, [in Fort Polk in Louisiana]. That is when this colonel showed up for the event and loved country music. After hearing us, he told the general and had me play for the officers' ball a few weeks later; that's when I was selected to be in special services entertainment division. Later on, I organized a *bluegrass festival through special services and had Bill Monroe, the Stone Mountain Boys, the Southern Bluegrass Boys (myself and Travis Stewart, Dennis Lucas and Gene Alford) and the Cumberlands (Harold and Betty Thom and Jim Smoak). I remember the whole budget for that one-day event was $500.*[120]

In the late 1960s, Alan backed up Byron Berline on guitar at numerous fiddle contests. It was at a fiddle contest in Fort Worth that Alan met Wayne Stewart and Sam Bush. Wayne encouraged Alan to move to Kentucky and form a band. So, after graduating from the University of Oklahoma, Alan headed east.

Wayne Stewart had this idea for a group with this kid he knew in Kentucky named Sam Bush, who was probably fifteen. So, I moved to Hopkinsville, Kentucky, and we formed Poor Richard's Almanac. Not long after, I got my draft notice, but before I left, Sam, Wayne and I made this tape, later released by Ridge Runner Records, called Poor Richard's Almanac. That was a lot of the instrumental things we were doing. I then went back to Oklahoma, was rejected by the army and worked in Norman that summer.[121]

In 1969, Alan heard that the king of bluegrass, Jimmy Martin, was short a banjo player. Alan auditioned, and before the week was out, he was on the road as one of the "Sunny Mountain Boys."

Alan would stay with Jimmy Martin for two years, realizing in 1971 that he needed to make a change.

Although Jimmy paid the $35 a day, a union minimum, we just didn't work enough to ever get ahead money-wise. I worked other jobs—substitute teacher, painting, pumping gas and a few pick-up music gigs. I think my total income each year I was with him was just over $2,000 (including other jobs), which translates to around $13,000 in current dollars. Although I was too naive to have worried about the lack of money, I slowly came around to realizing it was not going to work for me. I enjoyed the challenge of the music making he required, but just couldn't make it on that little bit of money.[122]

Alan wrote a letter to Byron Berline that he was looking to make a change. Berline was in California, playing with Dillard and Clark and the Flying Burrito Brothers.

Byron wrote back, encouraging Alan to come to California, as they were starting a band, which would become Country Gazette. However, before he could pack up and head to California, Byron called the boardinghouse where Alan lived. There was a change of plan—would Alan consider heading to Europe as a Flying Burrito Brother? Alan met the rest of the band at the airport in New York.

The Burritos had just released *Last of the Red-Hot Burritos*; however, Chris Hillman and Al Perkins left the band to join Stephen Stills's Manassas project. With a European tour booked and not wanting to lose any money, the promoter asked Berline to put together a band to perform as the Burrito Brothers. The European press referred to them as the "Fake Burrito Brothers"; the band's dynamic musicianship won them over.

After the European tour, Alan, Byron Berline, Roger Bush and Kenny Wertz formed the Country Gazette in 1972, a band that Alan would lead in multiple configurations for the next twenty years.

In 1986, Alan started teaching at South Plains College in Levelland, Texas. His Country Gazette bandmate Joe Carr had started teaching at the college in 1984. "Teaching was a natural development for Alan; he was writing monthly columns for *Banjo Newsletter* and *Frets*, and pre-concert workshops had been a regular feature of Country Gazette performances since 1977."[123] Alan would stay at South Plains until he retired from the school in 2007. During these two decades, Alan would remain prolific in his musical output.

Alan and Joe Carr formed a duo, creating what they referred to as "border bluegrass," or bluegrass with a hint of Tex-Mex. The Alan Munde–Joe Carr collaboration would also result in the book *Prairie Nights to Neon Lights: The Story of Country Music in West Texas*, the two-man musical comedy play *Two Swell Guys from Texas* and a critically acclaimed album, *Welcome to West Texas*. In 2008, Alan and Joe Carr received Lifetime Achievement Awards from the International Bluegrass Music Association.

In 2004, Alan formed the formed the Alan Munde Gazette. Then, in 2006, Alan was elected to the board of the International Bluegrass Music Association. Also during these two decades, Country Gazette albums, solo albums and instructional books were released.

After relocating to Wimberly, Texas, Alan started Alan Munde's Banjo College.[124] Munde also continued collaborating and creating music. He formed a performing trio with guitarist Elliott Rogers and bassist Janice Rogers called Ranch Road 12.

He also performed and recorded with mandolinist Billy Bright's Two High String Band. This friendship with Bright would result in two critically

Top: Alan Munde (*left*) and Byron Berline in Denver, 1983. *Photograph courtesy of Rick Gardner.*

Bottom: Country Gazette, in 2016, celebrating Alan Munde's seventieth birthday. *Left to right*: Byron Berline, Alan Munde, Roger Bush and Roland White. *Photograph courtesy of Rick Gardner.*

acclaimed albums: *Bright Munde* in 2014 and *Es Mi Suerte* in 2018. Speaking of their first collaboration, Alan said:

> *Billy and I live within a few miles of each other in Wimberley, Texas, in what is known as the Hill Country. We've played together on many local gigs for several years and enjoyed the shared experience of music making.*

The first two Alan Munde and Billy Bright albums. *Photograph courtesy of Jeff Campbell.*

We agreed to try to set some of our ideas down in a recording and began our project with a relaxed and casual schedule, only recording when we were ready with a tune.[125]

Alan reflected on his experience with bluegrass in the Lone Star State: "Every metro area had a bluegrass scene that was nourishing and rewarding. The music exists because people want it and want to play it. Because they love it.

As a master musician with over fifty years of prolific output and diverse collaborations, how does Alan Munde define bluegrass? "Bluegrass is a winding river with two defined banks. Sometimes, the river floods, and that's a good thing, like the flooding of the Nile or Euphrates would enrich the soil and irrigate.[126]

PETER ROWAN: THE TEXAS YEARS

Peter Rowan earned his bluegrass stripes playing in Bill Monroe's band. Keen and Rowan lived near each other in Nashville in the 1980s before both relocated to the Texas Hill Country around 1990. Keen remembers a colorful detail about Rowan from that time: "He was staying at my house in Bandera, thinking about buying a house in Texas. He was sitting

there, looking at a map, and he was going, 'Blaaahn-co, Blaaahn-co. Muh-deee-na, Muh-deee-na.' I asked him what he was doing, and he said, 'I'm just trying to figure out what town sounds the best.'" Rowan eventually chose Blanco.[127]
—Peter Blackstock

So, how did a Boston-born bluegrass boy end up in Texas for twenty-five years? Those seeds were first planted in San Antonio, Texas. After leaving Bill Monroe's band, Rowan's musical journey had taken him down one thousand roads. He first formed the Bluegrass Dropouts with David Grisman, then the Earth Opera and then Sea Train (1969–1972) with Richard Greene and drummer Roy Blumenfeld.

It was with Sea Train that Rowan grew weary of the life of a touring musician. With only a few dates left on their tour, Rowan decided to leave the band. The last three shows for Rowan took place in Houston, San Antonio and the last show was in Washington, D.C., a week later.

The morning after the Houston show, Rowan took a walk through the neighborhood. He was struck by two things: the mix of Latinos and White people and the contrast of his then-current lifestyle. After the San Antonio

PETER ROWAN

Photo Credit: Amanda Rowan

Peter Rowan. *Photograph courtesy of Amanda Rowan.*

show, he told the band he was staying for the week and would meet them in Washington, D.C., for his last concert with the band.

"The morning after the Houston show, I walked around and noticed people on their porch, friendly, White and Hispanic. It was so down-home and a contrast with the rock and roll lifestyle."[128] The Houston experience led to his decision to spend a week in Old San Antone.

> *I spent my time wandering the streets. You could hear Conjunto music and community choirs. There was a taqueria that sold tacos, two for $1.25, but you had to go next door to the pool hall to buy a beer. I was struck by the simplicity compared to the grind of the music business, set lists and traveling.*
>
> *I wandered to the westside and its wooden buildings. I heard a trumpet coming from one. There, on a rickety stage, were three musicians: accordion, trumpet and snare drum. Not bluegrass but similar to bluegrass in using the instruments at hand. I was the only "gringo" there. It was my first experience with another culture.*[129]

After a week in San Antonio, Rowan's musical path eventually led him to Nashville. However, the call of the Lone Star State would eventually lead him back.

Texas singer/songwriter Robert Earl Keen had moved to Nashville in 1986. Rowan explains how their friendship developed: "Robert lived just down the street from me, and we had a mutual friend in Ken Levitan (manger for Lyle Lovett, Nanci Griffith and New Grass Revival). We became soul mates and even wrote together. Robert had a regular gig at the Station Inn but couldn't find footing here and went back to Texas."[130]

Also, Rowan had met Hank Harrison, the band leader for the San Antonio–based group Tennessee Valley Authority. Through jamming and developing a friendship with the TVA, Rowan met Flaco Jimenez, the Texas accordion king. Rowan and Jimenez gigged around Austin. They also recorded two albums together: *San Antonio Sound* in 1983 and *Live Rockin' Tex-Mex* in 1984.

In 1990, Rowan made the move to Texas, purchasing what he described as a "two-room shack in Blanco." He continued, "Texas was an escape from the mundane of Nashville. A place

Peter Rowan. *Photograph courtesy of Tim Benko.*

to grow personally. You could hear the sound of cattle and every Tuesday morning; there was a livestock auction that started at 5:30 a.m. There were neighbors talking over the fence."[131]

In Texas, Rowan had the chance to rekindle friendships with musicians like Junior Brown and Robert Earl Keen. Junior Brown is famous for his guit-steel, a combination guitar and steel guitar. Rowan was there when Brown debuted the instrument in Nashville in 1985:

> *I had to sit down and play it on my lap, because I hadn't invented a stand for it yet. The gig was at the Station Inn, a popular bluegrass club in Nashville, and I played with Peter Rowan. Vince Gill sang that night with us, Mark O'Connor played fiddle, Jerry Douglas was on dobro and Roy Husky Jr. was on bass. It was a very high-profile gig, and I walked onstage and started playing the thing like I'd been doing it for fifty years.*[132]

Rowen lent his talents to Robert Earl Keen's 2015 bluegrass album, *Happy Prisoner, the Bluegrass Sessions*. Rowan is featured on the song "99 Years for One Dark Day" and also contributes the highlight of the album, a haunting introduction to the song "Walls of Time," which Rowan wrote with Bill Monroe.

In 1997, Rowan received a Grammy Award for his work on the album *True Life Blues: The Songs of Bill Monroe*. The album was awarded bluegrass album of the year.

Rowan formed the Texas Trio with Bryn Davies Bright (bass) and Billy Bright (mandolin, Two High String Band/Wood & Wire) in 1999, after sharing the stage at the Old Settlers Music Festival. The band would tour across the country and with the Tony Rice. This would eventually lead to two albums: *You Were There for Me* in 2004 and *Quartet* in 2007. Sharon Gilchrist played mandolin on the *Quartet* album after the divorce of Bryn and Billy.

Billy Bright had previously joined Rowan for an album with Texas cowboy singer Don Edwards: the Grammy-nominated *High Lonesome Cowboy* (2002). The album also featured Norman Blake and Tony Rice.

In 2012, the Bluegrass Heritage Foundation awarded Rowan its Bluegrass Star Award. The award was given at the annual Bloomin' Bluegrass Festival in Farmers Branch, Texas.

During his time in Texas, Rowan would play multiple venues form Austin's Cactus Café to the Blanco Town Square. He would also produce a deep and diverse discography that ranged from "reggaebilly" in 2001 to 2017's "My Aloha!"

However, by 2017, the Texas Hill Country was changing, and Rowan made the move to Marin County, California. In an interview with the *Marin Independent Journal*, Rowan stated:

> *"You know, there's a great charm to the Texas hill country,"* he says. *"I went there for the less-hectic lifestyle than Nashville was offering at the time. And when you're there, you think it's the place to be. But it's gotten so crowded. The hills are limestone, so they keep putting in grapevines and wineries. People think it's the South of France."*[133]

Still, Rowan maintains his Texas ties. Max Bacca called Rowan in 2018 and suggested some Texas shows with his own Tex-Mex conjunction, Los TexManiacs; Peter reunited with Flaco for the Texas shows. "It was like old times," said Rowan. "Los TexManiacs are a modern progressive bunch of guys who grew up musically listening to what I played with Flaco. They know my songs, and they include me as part of their tradition!" The Free Mexican Airforce is flying again.[134]

In 2020, Rowan lent his famous yodel to the song "Roadies Circles." The song is on the Austin-based Wood & Wire's album *No Matter Where It Goes*.

7

A NEW MILLENNIUM

In the early 2000s, traditionally based acoustic music encountered a period of revival, primarily due to the overwhelming success of the film soundtrack *O Brother Where Art Thou*. The platinum-selling recording contained several bluegrass selections that influenced many up-and-coming musicians. During this period, two different Texas-based groups emerged on the national scene: the Greencards and Cadillac Sky.

In 2008, Alan Tompkins of Dallas would start the Bluegrass Heritage Foundation, a nonprofit organization that not only introduced other Texans to bluegrass through numerous festivals and concerts, but also helped get instruments into the hands of aspiring young musicians through the Play It Forward program.

Like other decades before it, the 2010s would bring forth several bands, such as Austin's Wood & Wire, that took their music outside of the typical confines. The Family Sowell, originally from Hempstead, were then in the process of honing their craft as a family unit, specializing in contemporary bluegrass alongside Gospel music. West Texas native Dave Walser would form a group that had bluegrass instrumentation but would pay tribute to the rock 'n' roll band that changed his life at the age of nine. While all of these artists are stylistically different from each other, they each have a strong fanbase, and each have carved out their own place in Texas bluegrass history.

Nate Lee (*right*) and Beck Buller (*with fiddle*) at the 2017 Bluegrass on Ballard Festival, Wylie, Texas. *Photograph courtesy of Jeff Campbell.*

Alan Tompkins and the Bluegrass Heritage Foundation

The Farmers Branch fest is one of my top two favorite bluegrass festivals,
and I've been to every one (except one) since they started.
—*Kenneth Brown, University of Texas*[135]

Without Alan Tompkins, bluegrass music wouldn't be as vibrant as it is in Texas today. He has brought many of the top bluegrass artists to the North Texas area over the years. There's no telling how many people were introduced to this music through the Bluegrass Heritage Foundation's various events.

The Bluegrass Heritage Foundation is responsible for the Bloomin' Bluegrass Festival in Farmers Branch, the Wylie Jubilee Bluegrass on Ballard, Bluegrass Saturday Night in McKinney, the Bluegrass Heritage Festival and the Play It Forward free instrument loaner program.

The roots of the Bluegrass Heritage Foundation go back to a soccer stadium in Frisco, Texas. The stadium opened in 2005, and at the time, it was one of the few soccer-specific stadiums in the country. The new stadium was partially financed by Lamar Hunt, who also owned the FC Dallas soccer club that would play in the stadium. Lamar Hunt, the owner of the Kansas City Chiefs and founder of the AFL, had a long history of supporting soccer. In 1967, he founded the Dallas Tornado professional soccer team.

As an employee to the Hunts, Alan Tompkins was tasked with bringing people and awareness to the new stadium north of Dallas. Alan, originally form Kentucky, had a passion for bluegrass. He decided to share that passion with North Texas. A proficient banjo and acoustic bass player, Alan worked with Gerald Jones to produce the first Frisco Bluegrass Festival.

The first Frisco Bluegrass Festival was held on October 22, 2006. The festival was headlined by Ricky Skaggs and Kentucky Thunder and featured Rhonda Vincent and the Rage, the Claire Lynch Band, Williams and Clark Expedition, Cadillac Sky and country singer Deryl Dodd.

The second Frisco Bluegrass Festival was held on October 6, 2007. The lineup included Rhonda Vincent and the Rage, Doyle Lawson and Quicksilver, the Lonesome River Band, Cadillac Sky, Beatlegrass and Carrie Hassler and Hard Rain.

Although the festivals brought first-class bluegrass to North Texas, neither festival was profitable. The decision was made to discontinue hosting bluegrass festivals at the new Frisco stadium. Alan did receive permission from the powers that be to start a bluegrass nonprofit and to use the Frisco festival's database of fans.

The Bluegrass Heritage Foundation was formed in 2008. Over the next few years, events would be held at the Sons of Herman Hall in Dallas, Arlington and Argyle.

The 2006 Frisco Bluegrass Festival at Pizza Hut Park. *Photograph courtesy of Alan Thompkins.*

Kenny Smith (*with guitar*) at the 2016 Bloomin' Bluegrass Festival in Famers Branch, Texas. *Photograph courtesy of Jeff Campbell.*

Michael Cleveland and Flamekeeper at the 2019 Bluegrass Heritage Festival in Farmers Branch, Texas. *Photograph courtesy of Jeff Campbell.*

In 2010, working with the City of Farmers Branch, the Bloomin' Bluegrass Festival was born. Over the years, the event has hosted Sam Bush, Hot Rize, Simon Flory, Sierra Hull, Ricky Skaggs and Kentucky Thunder, Del McCoury Band, Travelin' McCourys, Rhonda Vincent and the Rage, Jerry Douglas and the Earls of Leicester, Molly Tuttle, Balsam Range, David Grisman, Peter Rowan, J.D. Crowe and the New South, Lonesome River Band, Russell Moore and IIIrd Tyme Out, the Seldom Scene, Michael Cleveland and Flamekeeper and many more.

The Bloomin' Bluegrass Festival has become the capstone of the Bluegrass Heritage Foundation's work. Along with the Bluegrass Heritage Festival and the Wylie, Texas Bluegrass on Ballard.

BLUE VALLEY BLUEGRASS

Blue Valley was a band based out of Rowlett, Texas. Their main run was from 2003 to 2010. The band consisted of Earl Clark on mandolin and lead vocals, Buzz Busby on bass, Mike Clark on guitar and harmony vocals and Joe Morrow on banjo and harmony vocals.

In 2005, the band released a self-made CD, *Bona Fide!* It's a hidden gem of an album, and mandolin player Braeden Paul considers it his favorite album by a Texas bluegrass band. "Hands down *Bona Fide!* by Blue Valley. I about wore that one out when I was younger and still listen to it some today."[136]

In the autumn of 2013, Buzz Busby and Joe Morrow decided they wanted to get the band back together. Earl Clark was dealing with significant health

Blue Valley Bluegrass. *From left to right*: Joe Morrow, Buzz Busby, Mike Clark and Earl Clark. *From the author's collection.*

issues, so Braeden Paul got the call to play mandolin. Other new additions were Pamela Dahl and Robby Paul on dobro. The reconfigured five-piece band was named Blue Valley Tradition. The new band name both differentiated them from and paid respect to the original band. The band played a handful of shows over the next two years. Their last performance was at the 2015 Bluegrass Heritage Foundation Front Porch Bluegrass Showdown in Dallas.

NATE LEE

In the small town of Ovilla, Texas, there lived a family of nine. The father, Chuck Lee, was a plumber by trade. In his spare time, he really enjoyed playing the banjo, specifically the clawhammer style of playing, which predates the popular three-finger style. In 2000, he ordered a banjo from a small custom shop. After two years of waiting and not receiving the completed instrument, Lee began converting a storage unit on his property into a workshop, where he completed his first hand-built banjo in April 2002. Every immediate member of the Lee family played music as a hobby. One of Lee's children, Nate, had a keen musical interest from an early age. Eventually, he would find himself drawn to the bluegrass genre.

> *My first exposure to bluegrass came in the form of cassette tapes brought home by my older brother. The first time I saw players like Alison Krauss, Dan Tyminski and John Hartford was when the Down From the Mountain tour took place, after the success of the movie O Brother Where Art Thou. I didn't get to see the show live, but my dad bought it on VHS, and we watched it over and over.* [137]

Nate Lee's musical journey began when he received his first fiddle at the age of eight. He started out taking violin lessons from a local teacher who specialized in the Suzuki method. Lee eventually started learning basic songs in the bluegrass repertoire, thanks, in part, to *Mel Bay's Easiest Fiddling Book*, written by Craig Duncan. His violin instructor was kind enough to help him learn different selections from the book, many of which Nate would eventually go on to perform. According to Lee, "They weren't explicitly bluegrass songs, but they were fiddle tunes that are often played in bluegrass, such as 'Liza Jane' and 'Sally Goodin.'" [138] Later on, Nate began learning how to play other instruments, such as the mandolin and guitar. He also learned how to play the banjo, specifically focusing on the clawhammer style, much like his father had.

As he continued to progress in his instrumental abilities, Nate's attraction to bluegrass began to grow even more. What most stood out to him was the communal and improvisational nature of the genre:

> *Bluegrass music was very accessible to me, because it was easy to meet people I could play music with. There were public jams in the Dallas area, and the pickers always made me feel welcome. The improvisational nature of bluegrass is on the same level as jazz, and that really appealed to me once I started to reach technical proficiency on my instruments* [mandolin and fiddle].[139]

Nate soon began to publicly perform with some Dallas-based bands, such as Jim Paul Miller's Garland Square Pickers, Back Porch Tradition and the Mark Gorman Band. He also continued to take private lessons and attend various music camps. This would ultimately lead him to the next step in his journey.

Nate decided to further his musical education by attending South Plains College in Levelland, Texas. While his degree was in commercial music, Lee also took part in the college's bluegrass and country music program, which allowed him to study the genre at an even deeper level. During these developmental years, Nate had several important mentors, such as Joe Carr, Alan Munde, Ed Marsh and Steve Smith. He also largely credits his music theory professor, Dr. Sam Germany, with helping him to cultivate an understanding of music structure and composition that he has found will serve him well throughout his career.

During his second semester at South Plains, in 2006, Lee joined the Alan Munde Gazette as their fiddler and toured with them for the next six years. The band's sound was reminiscent of Munde's earlier group, the Country Gazette. This new configuration performed a combination of fresh, original material, as well as classic songs that had been part of the Country Gazette's repertoire from 1972 to 1991. Nate appeared on the group's 2008 release, *Made to Last*.

After the Alan Munde Gazette stopped touring, Nate filled in with different bands until he decided to take a respite from music. During this time, he studied to become a motorcycle mechanic. Eventually, Lee decided to return to his career as a musician, and in 2012, he made the move to Nashville, Tennessee.

Once he was settled in, Nate began performing with various groups around the Nashville area. He also found himself touring with different artists, such as Ashleigh Caudill, Brad Folk and the Bluegrass Playboys, Irene Kelley and Town Mountain.

In 2015, Nate was named the "Momentum Instrumentalist of the Year" by the International Bluegrass Music Association (IBMA). Also at this time, Lee was playing mandolin and fiddle alongside IBMA Award–winning guitar player Jim Hurst as part of the Jim Hurst Trio. The group released the album, *JHT-1* in 2016. During the course of this particular period, Lee would occasionally go on the road to be a substitute musician with the Becky Buller Band, a group that showcased the powerful singing, dynamic fiddling and unique original material of its Grammy-winning leader.

In 2017, Nate Lee joined the Becky Buller Band as a full-time member. He primarily served as the group's mandolinist but would occasionally pick up the fiddle for a few songs. This allowed him and Buller to incorporate their own brand of twin fiddling in their live stage performances. Lee appeared on two of Buller's recordings, *Crepe Paper Heart*, released in 2018, and *Distance and Time*, released in 2020.

Even though he found himself busy, performing in different live venues and recording in various studios, Nate always found time to pursue his greatest passion—teaching. Through teaching both at private lessons and at music camps whenever his schedule allowed, Lee has helped many aspiring instrumentalists hone their craft. He also expanded his music instruction to videos on YouTube, as well as the release of an instructional DVD, *How to Play a Solo on a Song You've Never Heard Before*, in 2018.

Nate has released two different solo recordings, the instrumental EP *Plays Well with Others* in 2017 and *Wings of a Jetliner* in 2020. Both projects feature strong supporting casts of acclaimed musicians, such as Jim Hurst, Ned Luberecki, Steve Smith, Wyatt Rice and Todd Phillips, among others.

CADILLAC SKY

Cadillac Sky, from Fort Worth, Texas, was active as a band from 2002 to 2011. Cadillac Sky definitely fell into the realm of progressive bluegrass. However, their first album on Ricky Skaggs's label, *Blind Man Walking* (2007), would be considered traditional bluegrass. Mandolinist Braeden Paul said:

I remember hearing Cadillac Sky play at Pizza Hut Park in Frisco, Texas, when I was about twelve years old. I remember they were very loud, much to the dismay of the more traditional bluegrass fans in the audience. They definitely pushed boundaries with their music, and they did it fearlessly. [140]

The original band members were Ross Holmes (fiddle), Bryan Simpson (mandolin), Mike Jump, Matt Blaize (bass and vocals) and Matt Menefee (banjo). In 2010, guitarist Levi Lowrey replaced Bryan Simpson, who abruptly left the band in the middle of tour opening for Munford and Sons.

The band became known for its musical proficiency and harmonies. Greg Yost reviewed their performance at the 2008 Pickin' in the Panhandle Bluegrass Festival:

Getting the festivities started for the day was Cadillac Sky. This band, originally from Texas, has been turning heads over the last few years with two albums that stretch the parameters that define bluegrass. Led by the talented singer/mandolin player/songwriter Bryan Simpson, Cadillac Sky entertained the crowd with selections from its first two albums, 2007's Blind Man Walking *and* Gravity's Our Enemy, *the band's new release on the Skaggs Family Records label.*

Although the band has some talented pickers, the most striking aspect of Cadillac Sky's music is the group's harmonizing. Songs like the tender ballad "Homesick Angel" and the franticly calming "Insomniac Blues for Matthew" were two of best moments from the band's sets. Both highlighted the band's signature harmonies. [141]

For their third album, Cadillac Sky moved to Dualtone Records and collaborated with Dan Auerbach of the Black Keys, who produced the album. Auerbach encouraged the band to stretch out and push the boundaries on the new album, *Letter's in the Deep*. This album pushed the band fully into progressive/newgrass territory.

By this time, only two original members were left in the band, Ross Holmes and Matt Menefee. The new additions were David Mayfield on guitar and Andy Moritz on bass. But it was not long before the band members went their separate ways.

Ross Holmes and Matt Menefee would form the duo ChessBoxer, which became a trio with the addition of bassist Royal Masat. The trio backed up Warren Haynes on his Ashes and Dust tour and was also his opening act.

Ross Holmes has also performed with Bruce Hornsby, toured with Abigail Washburn and performed with Phil Collins on "Davy Crockett's Fiddle at the Alamo."

Bryan Simpson became a solo performer and songwriter; releasing two albums in 2014 and 2017. He has written hit songs for George Strait, Tim McGraw and numerous others.

THE GREENCARDS

There's a reason that Austin, Texas, is known as the "live music capital of the world." Austin is probably the only place that a guy from England and a guy and girl from Australia could form a progressive, American bluegrass band. That's the kind of thing that happens in the bars and music venues of Austin, Texas.

Eamon McLoughlin was born in London, England. The son of Irish parents, he grew up playing country music in the family's band. He first started playing the fiddle at the age of nine. After graduating from Sussex University with a degree in politics and American studies, he relocated to Austin, Texas.

In Australia, Kym Warner grew up in a home filled with bluegrass, as his father was an Australian bluegrass pioneer. The Australian Bluegrass Mandolin Championship crowned Kym a champion for four straight years. Carol Young sang in Australian country music bands, charting two number-one country singles in her native Australia. She was also nominated for best female vocalist by the Country Music Association of Australia and was 2000's Australian independent country artist of the year.

When Warner met Young, a singer in Outback country bands, the pair decided to immigrate to America and get serious about bluegrass. They spent some time in West Texas before moving to Austin to find a more hospitable environment. "I don't think they like foreigners too well," said Warner.[142]

Eamon, Kym and Carol met at a recording session. Kym Warner needed a fiddle player for an album she was producing for Bill Atkins, and Eamon answered the call. Three Austin immigrants started jamming and writing songs together. They chose the name the Greencards. The name of the band does not have an eccentric or odd meaning like Leftover Salmon or the String Cheese Incident. All three musicians had U.S. green cards, thus the name "the Greencards." Eamon McLoughlin said:

The ironic thing is that we grew up listening to primarily American music and fell in love with American music. I love country music. I grew up with George Jones and Charley Pride and Jim Reeves. All that stuff was playing in the house. That's what I wanted to seek out. That's what I wanted to play. Carol was into Tammy Wynette. Trev Warner is Kym's dad, and he was the first person to bring bluegrass music to Australia.[143]

Their first gig was at Mother Egan's, a now-defunct Irish pub that was on Sixth Street in Austin. Their new grass mix of Americana, gypsy jazz and Celtic influences caught on quickly with Austin music fans. Their crowds grew, and they opened shows for Robert Earl Keen. Soon, they recorded their first album.

In 2003, the band recorded their first album, *Movin' On*. The self-released album was critically acclaimed and attracted new fans to the band. In *Paste Magazine*, Brian Quincy Newcomb praised the band's instrumental virtuosity:

Instrumental romps like "Jolly Hockeysticks," "Small Tots," "Leonardo's Ride" and the mid-section of "You Pulled Me Out" find no problems in translation. Barnburner virtuoso solos on mandolin, fiddle and from guest guitarists reveal a grasp of the vernacular. Check out bassist Carol Young's voice drawl on the title track and Robert Earl Keen's "Love's a Word I Never Throw Around," and you'll be reminded accents are usually spoken, not sung. Her fellow Aussie, Kym Warner, and Brit Eamon McLaughlin trade vocals as well, and they've found a solid harmony footing with Young on Gillian Welch's "Caleb Meyer." But the Greencards' real power remains their stunning instrumental prowess[144]

In 2004, the band signed with Dualtone Records, which rereleased *Movin' On*, and they were also recognized as "best new band" at the Austin Music Awards. The year 2005 would find the band releasing another critically acclaimed album, *Weather and Water*. They would spend the summer opening shows for Bob Dylan and Willie Nelson on their minor league ballpark tour. In late 2005, the band also relocated their home base from Austin to Nashville.

From 2007 to 2011, the band would release three more albums: *Viridian* in 2007 on Dualtone, *Fascination* in 2009 on Sugar Hill and their self-financed "buy a brick" album appropriately titled *The Brick Album* in 2011.

Eamon would leave the band during the Christmas season of 2009 and lend his talents to Josh Turner, Ashley Monroe and the Bodeans. In 2016, he joined the band "Fifty Shades of Hay" and became the staff fiddler for the *Grand Ole Opry*.

The final Greencards album, *Sweethearts of the Sun*, was released in 2013. The band's tenure would produce three Grammy nominations in 2008, 2010 and 2014.

After their last album, Kym Warner would join bluegrass fan Robert Earl Keen's touring band, and Carol Young continued working professionally as an event planner, musician and hospitality professional.

HOT PICKIN' 57'S

Known as "Austin's favorite bluegrass band," the Hot Pickin' 57's formed in January 2016. That first year, the band traveled across the state, playing venues from Luckenbach to Grapevine's Grapefest.

The 57's are led by Max Zimmet, a graduate of the Berklee College of Music. Livingston Taylor said, "Max has an ability to focus and concentrate that is unique in the Berklee environment. Musically, Max is equally focused; a very compelling energy emerges as he plays that holds a class like a laser beam. To me, Max is the individual that makes Berklee such a special place."[145]

Max started taking classical guitar lessons at the age of eight. Two years later, he heard Bill Monroe on *Austin City Limits*. At his next guitar lesson, he asked his guitar instructor to teach him some Bill Monroe tunes. In Max's teenage years, he took lessons from John Moore, Bryan Sutton and Cody Kilby. In the Austin music scene, the person he worked with the most early on was Eddie Collins.

Other members of the band include Vance Hazen on bass, Michael Montgomery on fiddle and Shawn Spiars on banjo. Vance was born in Montana and raised in Ohio; he also collects vintage bicycles. Michael has a PhD in astronomy and started classical violin training at the age of ten. Shawn graduated with an associate degree in bluegrass music from South Plains College and has played with numerous bands across Central Texas.

As of 2020, the band has released a self-titled CD in 2017 and an EP, *Hot Picks*, in 2019.

When asked about the state of bluegrass in Texas, Max said, "We think the future is bright, as bluegrass music seems to be getting more and more popular, not only in Texas, but around the world." When asked if he could change one thing about the bluegrass community, he said, "If we're

Max Zimmet (*with guitar*) and the Hot Pickin' 57's. *Photograph courtesy of Max Zimmet.*

talking about the Texas bluegrass community, I would say that there is a component of the community that only views very traditional bluegrass as true bluegrass. I like the broader view such as can be seen in festivals like Merlefest and Rockygrass."[146]

THE FAMILY SOWELL

Although they would eventually make their home in Tennessee, the Sowell family would begin their musical journey in Hempstead, Texas, fifty miles west of Houston. Cindy and Guynn Sowell's six children, Jacob, Joshua, Naomi, Abigail, John-Mark and Justus, all began playing piano at a very young age.[147]

A family vacation soon allowed them to discover the music they would ultimately fall in love with. Abigail Sowell reflected:

> *We were first introduced to bluegrass music in 2006 while watching Rhonda Vincent and the Rage perform at Silver Dollar City's Bluegrass*

and Barbecue in Branson, Missouri. Seeing Kenny Ingram, who played with Rhonda at the time, Jacob immediately fell in love with the five-string banjo and wanted to learn.[148]

The Sowell family attended the Bluegrass and Barbecue Festival again the next year and also in 2009 and 2011. As they were learning more about the bluegrass genre, one aspect really stood out more than the rest. "We loved the family aspect of it, listening to groups like the Isaacs and Flatt Lonesome, among others, and we wanted to bring our own sense of family and spin of bluegrass back to the Houston area."[149]

The Sowell siblings' first performance experience did not come from playing bluegrass; it came from playing jazz and big band–era music on tenor banjos with the ALLSTARS, a youth banjo band that was formed at Sagemont Church in Houston. The group's director, Buddy Griffin, noticed how rapidly the Sowells were developing their musical abilities. He soon encouraged them to form their own band, which they did in October 2010. They named themselves the Sowell Family Pickers. The new group started performing at local events, several of which were referrals by Griffin whenever he was unable to make a show.

As the Sowells were first developing their sound, they were influenced by various bluegrass and gospel artists. Abigail Sowell stated they particularly admired "groups like the Isaacs, Rhonda Vincent and the Rage, Dailey and Vincent, Ricky Skaggs, Doyle Lawson and Quicksilver to name a few. In

These six siblings make up the Family Sowell. Jacob (banjo), John-Mark (fiddle), Joshua (guitar), Naomi (bass), Abigail (mandolin) and Justus (resonator guitar). *Photograph courtesy of the Family Sowell.*

later years, Alison Krauss and Union Station made a *huge* impact on our arrangement and approach to our music and creative thought process. They all played their role in shaping our love of bluegrass music and helped lay a good foundation to build upon in developing our own unique style." They also received mentorship from different people, such as vocal coach Vicki Wehmeyer, fiddlers Greg Bailey (formerly a member of Loretta Lynn's band) and Robert Herridge (formerly with Johnny Lee).

For the next several years, the family continued performing at local churches and other venues. At the time, they primarily viewed music as a fun hobby they could all do together. In 2016, the Sowells made the decision to make music their livelihood. They ultimately sold their home in Hempstead and moved to Knoxville, Tennessee, allowing themselves to be more connected to the bluegrass music industry. Soon, they would gain mentorship from various industry professionals, such as Stephen Mougin, Ben Issacs and Jerry Salley.

The year 2017 would prove to be a monumental one for the Sowells. Along with the move to Knoxville, the group released two studio recordings, *Shadowlands* and the Christmas collection *Best Gift Of All.*[150] In May of that same year, the Sowells came full circle when they were named the winners of the KSMU Youth in Bluegrass Competition, which was held at Silver Dollar City's Bluegrass and Barbecue Festival, the same location where they discovered the genre eleven years earlier.

In 2018, the Sowells took some bigger steps in their musical journey. The first was changing their name from the Sowell Family Pickers to the Family Sowell. They would release one final recording under the Sowell Family Pickers name, *Trust in the Lord.* Their first studio project under the Family Sowell moniker was *From Texas to Tennessee* on Poor Mountain Records. They eventually got opportunities to perform at prestigious events and at venues such as ROMP Fest in Owensboro, Kentucky, and Dollywood in Pigeon Forge, Tennessee. The Family Sowell also had the opportunity to share their music in different countries, such as Serbia, Romania, Montenegro, Hungary and Israel.[151]

More recordings and accolades followed for the Family Sowell. In 2019, they won the Society for Preservation of Bluegrass Music in America (SPBGMA) International Band Championship. In 2020, they released several recordings, including the album *Same Kind of Different*; the single "Love Is the Key"; a gospel EP, *Worship with the Fam*; and a second Christmas project, titled *K-Town Christmas.* In 2021, the group released *Time Travel with the Family Sowell.*[152]

SGT. PEPPER'S LONELY BLUEGRASS BAND

On Sunday February 9, 1964, a group of four men from Liverpool, England, known as the Beatles made their debut appearance on the *Ed Sullivan Show*. Viewed by an estimated audience of 73 million, this performance not only heightened the group's popularity but changed the course of American music history. One of these viewers was a young boy in West Texas. In the years to come, he would honor the Beatles in a way that was completely divergent from others who recognized their legacy.

Dave Walser's interest in music began at the age of six. His father, who avidly listened to bluegrass music decided to take up the guitar. Shortly thereafter, Dave decided to learn to play as well. Music making ultimately became a fun hobby for Walser and his father to take part in together.[153]

Just a few short years later, Dave saw the Beatles on the *Ed Sullivan Show*. Captivated by the group's unique sound, it quickly influenced the direction of his musical journey. Walser would soon start playing his own renditions of Beatles songs. In 2002, Dave had the opportunity to see Paul McCartney in concert during his Back in the U.S. tour. Inspired by this performance, an idea began to form in Walser's head of combining acoustic instrumentation with material that had been recorded and popularized by the Beatles.[154]

The idea would finally come to fruition in 2004, when Dave formed the trio, Beatlegras. The group consisted of Walser on guitar; Milo Deering,

Sgt. Pepper's Lonely Bluegrass Band at the 2017 Bluegrass on Ballard Festival, Wylie, Texas. *Photograph courtesy of Jeff Campbell.*

who played mandolin, along with several other instruments; and George Anderson on bass.[155] For the next seven and a half years, Beatlegrass would perform at different venues around Texas and other parts of the United States. They also released three different albums.

In 2011, Beatlegrass decided to take a year off to focus on other artistic ventures. A year later, Dave Walser decided to reform the group, this time, with a new name and new members. Now known as Sgt. Pepper's Lonely Bluegrass Band, this four-piece ensemble consisted of players from various musical backgrounds.[156] Along with Walser, the new configuration consisted of Gerald Jones on banjo and mandolin; fiddler Reginald Rueffer, who formerly toured with the late country singer Charley Pride; and jazz bassist Bach Norwood. Sgt. Pepper's would eventually go on to tour in various parts of the United States. In 2016, the group released a self-titled studio recording. Produced by Dave Walser, the album consists of ten Beatles classics, among them, "Here Comes the Sun," "Blackbird" and "Eleanor Rigby."

BILLY BRIGHT

El Paso brings to mind Southwest culture, Mexican food and mariachis. El Paso is also the birthplace oof one of America's top mandolin players, Billy Bright. Billy's geographic journey took him from El Paso to Boston and then to Austin. His musical journey took him from punk rock to bluegrass. Billy explained the link from the punk rock world to bluegrass:

> *The link for me was just a musical evolution wrapped into my own journey and discovery. I was open to any kind of music that fell on my ears the right way. Punk is perfect for teenage years, almost handcrafted for that, based purely on feeling and raw emotions and lots of cursing and mostly incomprehensible lyrics. Bluegrass is the punk rock of the country music world…and has been since day one. Is there anything more punk than Bill Monroe? Rolf Sieker even told me once, "There is nothing more punk than Bill Monroe." As I have gotten older and still enjoy many of the sounds of my youth, I see more similarities than differences between the two. Sure, on the surface, they are vastly different. But within the feeling and the message of the music—very similar. Both of these "styles" are in the DIY fringes of the "music industry" (and always have been) and are mostly performed by folks who are going to be doing it whether they "make a living" doing it or not, i.e., they don't give a **** about conforming to any "mainstream:*

December 13, 2019, Wood & Wire playing at the Trail of Lights, Zilker Park, Austin, Texas. *Photograph courtesy of Natalie Turner.*

> *industry protocols. And all the fans all have their own bands and play, too. And there is a "one of us" feeling amongst the fans and the bands because we are all one in the same.*[157]

Billy also discussed his brother's influence on his musical knowledge growing up:

> *I can credit almost all my knowledge of music, musicians, and styles of music, to my brother, Ben. We were certainly of the early MTV generation, back when the "M" was for music....Ben's pursuits to get all the good stuff that wasn't available at the record store led us to the Headstand—a "headshop" that also sold all the "indie" records (before it was called "indie") and imports and bootlegs, etc. Anything you could not find at Sound Warehouse, they had there, from punk to psychedelic rock, the goriest death metal, to country, bluegrass, and Tejano. So, naturally, when my punk interests led to hard rock, which led to psychedelic rock, Neil Young, Hot Tuna, and the Grateful Dead, the Garcia/Grisman record came out...and the Bad Livers' Delusion of Banjer (hands down best album title ever). That pretty much did it for me. Paved the road right to Monroe and the two John's—Duffy and Hartford.*[158]

Billy would enroll at the Berklee College of Music in Boston, Massachusetts. Berklee, established in 1945, is the world's largest independent college of independent music. Some of the famous alumni of Berklee include Al Di Meola, Donald Fagen, Bill Frisell, Bruce Hornsby, Sierra Hull, Quincy Jones, Branford Marsalis, Natalie Maines and John Scofield. Billy talks about his time and motivation while at Berklee:

> *I was at Berklee back when there was no bluegrass or mandolin instruction. My roommate then, and now brother-in-law, Brian Smith came from bluegrass family in Pennsylvania, and he was the first person I met who could play and sing all the songs. I eventually got to go to Pennsylvania with him and become part of his bluegrass family and have my first experience playing real bluegrass with a truck driver, Wayne (who had been struck by lightning twice), on the banjo and Brian's granddad Blain on the fiddle. Brian and I had picked every night in our dorm, then our apartment in Boston, found the bluegrass community there at the Cantab Lounge in Cambridge with Geoff Bartley and eventually formed Two High String Band there in 1995. I went to Berklee with one goal…to meet people and start a band. I was in way over my head from the start. I was one of the few people there who had not been studying music for years already. I would never have even considered a performance degree track. When I had to choose my major, I chose music business because I thought that would be more helpful than anything when starting a band. I remember in the recording contract class, in 1995, they were talking about all this distribution stuff and royalties, etc., talking about how the whole business is laid out. Somebody said, "What about the internet?" The professor said they had heard about the internet and that it might change things a little bit.*[159]

Billy would eventually return to Texas, but his destination was Austin, not El Paso. He said:

> *Well, family in Austin was a big draw. Beyond that, the Bad Livers and the earliest incarnations of the Asylum Street Spankers had a deep impact on my musical experience. My motivation to go to college was to find people to play in a band in Austin with. I had spent a lot of time in Nashville. I had lived in the Northeast. Austin was just what fit me.*[160]

Back in Austin, Billy would form the Two High String Band and find himself collaborating with two of the biggest names in bluegrass: Peter

Rowan and Tony Rice, thanks to Keith Case. Keith Case, who passed away in 2019, was a talent agent, manager and promoter. Through the years, he worked with not only Rice and Rowan but also Ralph Stanley, the Nashville Bluegrass Band, Peter Rowan, Hot Rize, Pete Wernick, Tim and Mollie O'Brien, the Seldom Scene, New Grass Revival, Sierra Hull and Highway 111, Rhonda Vincent, Ronnie Bowman, the Del McCoury Band and the Steep Canyon Rangers.

> *I was already a fan of Peter's when I met him at the Cactus Café in Austin, thanks to Cash Edwards. We crossed paths several times after that, and I eventually got a call from Keith Case about doing a tour in September '99. After that tour, as I've heard Peter explain, he asked me what my future held, and when I told him I had no future, he knew we were going to work together. And after that, the calls from Keith kept coming.*

Billy would spend the next five years working with Peter Rowan and Tony Rice, not only touring, but also in the recording studio. Billy would play mandolin on the album *High Lonesome Cowboy*. *High Lonesome Cowboy* featured Peter Rowan, cowboy songster Don Edwards and the guitar virtuosos Tony Rice and Norman Blake. The album would win best traditional folk album at the forty-fifth Grammy Awards. Billy would also lend his mandolin and mandola to the Peter Rowan and Tony Rice album *You Were There for Me*. Billy described working with Tony Rice: "It was like apprenticing with a quiet and kind anomalous master of his craft."[161]

During this time, Billy would also teach mandolin to a very young Sarah Jarosz. Sarah would grow up to become an acclaimed American singer/songwriter.

> *Living in the same small town, going to Mike Bond's bluegrass jam, Sarah and I met when she was nine, and her folks asked me to start giving her lessons almost immediately, which led to her sitting in with the Two High String Band all the time as well as eventually doing a bunch of duo work. Then the student becomes the teacher.*

Billy and his fellow Berklee alumnus Brian Smith (guitar) had been playing off and on with the Two High String Band since 1995. Geoff Union (guitar) joined the band on 2002 and the band became a fulltime endeavor. In 2003, the band released their first album, *Insofarasmuch*.

In 2006, the core of Bright, Smith and Union would remain. However, the band added Tony Trischka's banjo excellence, Eric Thorin on bass and Wayne "Chojo" Jacques on fiddle for the album *Moonshine Boogie*. Billy loved collaborating with Chojo: "Loved Chojo's playing from back when he was the Waybacks. Used to do a lot of duo tours with him as a duo, and then we put a band together with Pat Manske and Mike Morgan, the Waynebillies. Best band name ever, but we never got to get the ball rolling 'cause real life took over!"[162]

In 2009, the band would add Alan Munde on banjo, Bad Livers cofounder Mark Rubin on bass and fiddler Erik Hokkanen, releasing the album *Hot Texas Bluegrass Burrito*. In a review by the *Austin Chronicle*'s Jim Caligiuri, the album received four and a half stars.

Though the Two High String Band never had an official breakup, the core three went in different directions. Geoff Union would head to the mountains of Colorado and start the band Ragged Union, while Brian Smith would relocate to Fort Worth and teach music.

The year 2014 would bring Billy two new collaborative projects with Alan Munde and the band Wood & Wire. He would record two duo albums with Alan Munde: 2014's *Bright Munde* and 2018's *Es Mi Suerte*.

> *Alan joined up with Two High String Band for our last record and last couple years of playing regionally here in Texas. Then we played together in RR12 and Alan Munde Gazette but eventually started recording duo records....Alan's idea, and are presently working on our third. Alan is the top of the top, not only as a musician, but as a mentor and human being in general. I am very grateful for this relationship.*

In 2014, Billy would join Austin based Wood & Wire. "Our directions collided at a moment when I was ready to do some gigging, and there was a need for mandolin. We got together to do some gigs in June 2014, and I never left!"[163] Since Billy joined the band, they have released two albums: 2018's Grammy-nominated *North of Despair* and 2020's *No Matter Where It Goes from Here*.

Billy's goal "to find people to play in a band in Austin with" has definitely been met.

WOOD & WIRE

The foundation of Wood & Wire was laid when singer/songwriter guitarist Tony Kamel and mandolinist Matt Slusher met in 2010. Both musicians had played with other bands, and Tony and Matt started jamming together. When bassist Dominic Fisher joined the jams, Wood & Wire formed as a trio. Later that year, banjo player Trevor Smith from the band Green Mountain Grass joined the group.

The band quickly built a following in Austin, with their driving, high-energy shows. By 2013, they were touring with Colorado's Yonder Mountain String and released their first album, the self-titled *Wood & Wire*.

Matt Slusher would move on to other musical projects, and mandolinist Billy Bright would join the band in 2014. Billy was well known by the other band members. Billy's band, the Two High String Band, had toured with Trevor's band, Green Mountain Grass. Dominic had played bass on an album Billy produced, and Tony had taken mandolin lessons from Billy.

Before Billy joined the band, the trio of Fisher, Smith and Kamel recorded their second album, *The Coast*. The recording's featured guests included Jason Carter, a member of the Travelin' McCourys and the Del McCoury Band and Andy Leftwich. The album was released in February 2015.

The music blog *Twangville* concluded its review of *The Coast* with this paragraph:

> *Overall, a lot of the songs on* The Coast *are just well written, well played traditional-sounding bluegrass songs. Which is sort of like saying becoming a concert pianist just takes practice. Wood & Wire is one of the finest bluegrass groups in the country today: take a listen to* The Coast, *and I think you'll agree.*[164]

The next album would see multiple "firsts": the first recording to feature Billy Bright, their first album with Austin's Blue Corn Music and their first Grammy nomination.

In 2018 the band's album *North of Despair* received a Grammy nomination for bluegrass album of the year. The nomination was totally unexpected by the band. Tony Kamel was still in bed when he got the Friday morning news:

> *"It wasn't even on my radar that the Grammy nominations had come out this morning," Kamel told* Playback *last night. "I got a text from my friend Matt in Nashville saying 'Congratulations.' I wrote back, 'Awww, thanks*

Left: An early performance by Wood & Wire, featuring Matt Slusher on mandolin. *Photograph courtesy of Tony Kamel.*

Below: Wood & Wire performing at the Historic Scoot Inn. *Photograph courtesy of Tony Kamel.*

man. She's stuck with me now,' thinking he was congratulating me for getting married. Then he said, 'Nah, you idiot—on the nomination!' I said, 'The nomination for what?' He said, 'For the big G—the Grammy!'"[165]

Billy Bright stressed the surrealness of being nominated for a Grammy:

It seemed to come out of nowhere, that's for sure! It was fun to receive some recognition and neat to see all the "academy" does behind the curtain. As far as perceptions go, I'm not sure. It seemed to be sort of a feather in the cap in the music business world. I guess, for some folks, it may be some sort of validation. I think, especially in the folk "aural" traditional music, what is surreal about it is being included with all the other "styles" of music, where it is all just "music." Especially for those of us who remember loving "bluegrass" pre-O Brother, etc., it's just surreal to be included in anything![166]

In 2020, the band followed up "North of Despair" with the album *North of Despair*. The year 2020 will forever be remembered for COVID-19 and its related impacts on society. Concert tours came to a halt, while some album releases were delayed, and other artists released "pandemic albums." Billy Bright talks about releasing an album during a once-in-a-century pandemic:

That was a release time that we had determined before the pandemic was even a consideration. The decision to not delay the release, like so we could tour around it or something, was easy. In times like these, if you've got something to share that might give even a glimmer of light, it's important to get it out there. Blue Corn Music, our label, were very encouraging, as well. They really wanted to get it out there, too.[167]

Lyrically the band has always stretched out with topics not typically associated with traditional bluegrass, like Mexico and the sea wall. That continues on *North of Despair*; a prime example is the first single off the album, "Pigs," written by Tony Kamel.

It's a social commentary, for sure—mostly around money. Money, divisive profit-driven news cycles, profits over people, constant consumption and waste—you know all of those uplifting modern hypocrisies. I wrote the tune a few years back after seeing a few things on TV that bothered me: a few ridiculous moments from a reality TV show and a video of a TV evangelist trying to convince his congregation to help him buy a new private jet, and of course some divisive news show. It touches on the biblical concept of "wolves in sheep's clothing" (Matthew 7:15).[168]

Another stand-out track is "My Hometown." Now, of course, there are lots of bluegrass songs about hometowns, but this is probably the first one about El Paso. The song was written by Billy Bright:

Well, when it comes to writing songs and genres, it sort of a chicken-before-the-egg kind of situation. It's true, most bluegrass songs, possibly no bluegrass songs, are about El Paso. That said, El Paso was my "little cabin

Wood & Wire at the Grammy Awards. *Photograph courtesy of Tony Kamel.*

home on the hill," just at the bottom of the hill was the Rio Grande. Instead of "revenue man" and "moonshine," you had "gangs" and "narcotics." The concept of "home," and the feeling of "home" is a recurring theme in bluegrass. Yet, less and less of the people performing string music these days make moonshine with the old folks at home in that little cabin home in Caroline. I've experimented with writing songs like that, and in the end, I feel very inauthentic to myself. I see songwriting as independent of style. Any song can be bluegrassed at any point. In this case, I wrote this song never intending for it to be played in this, or any, band. So, it's journey into Wood & Wire's twist on bluegrass was pretty spur of the moment. We were seeking material, and Tony didn't have anything he wanted to contribute, so I dumped some of my songs out that I thought he might like singing, and now we have El Paso bluegrass!

The original origins of this song come from me hearing someone sing a song about their hometown on the radio. A song that was very of the americana Cracker Barrel sweet template…and I thought, "What would I say about my hometown?" Which got me thinking of the El Paso I left when I was nineteen and what it had been leading up to then. Thinking

Wood & Wire (*left to right*): Billy Bright, Tony Kamel, Dominic Fisher and Trevor Smith. *Photograph courtesy of Tony Kamel.*

about all the living I had done there—my story. Thinking about all the stuff that had happened since I left; what had happened to my friends and the music scene. El Paso has always been a unique and extreme place. The beauty of people and geography matched with the dark brutality of humanity wedged between the mountains of two different countries. The 1980s, when I grew up there, El Paso was left alone—out on the range. As kids, we went freely from the United States to Mexico and back—without parental supervision. Gang laws. Civilians were safe.

However, on a side note, Billy points out a strange coincidence. Wood & Wire cannot claim to be "first" when it comes to El Paso bluegrass:

When I discovered the mail order catalog by Janet Davis Music in the early '90s it was a godsend to be able to get accessories that an acoustic musician would want to mail order, pre-internet, in El Paso. When I got my first order from her, I saw her return address in EL Paso, where she was living at the time. I was able to go pick some stuff up from her in person after that.[169]

Wood & Wire's music not only resonates with bluegrass fans, but they also attract fans from the Texas Red Dirt scene and the jamgrass crowd. Their original, well-crafted songs and driving, high-energy shows have wide appeal.

NOTES

A Special Thanks to the Pickin' Singin' Professor

1. Rod Moag, www.rodmoag.home.texas.net.

Howdy Forrester Went Down to Texas

2. Cecelia Tichi, *Reading Country Music: Steel Guitars, Opry Stars and Honky Tonk Bars* (Durham, NC: Duke University Press, 1998), 362.
3. Neil V. Rosenberg, *Bluegrass: A History* (Champaign: University of Illinois Press, 2005), 55.
4. Ibid., 55, n15.
5. Bill Monroe, *Blue Moon of Kentucky 1936–1949*, Bear Family, 2003, 6 compact discs, 40.
6. Gayel Pitchford, *Fiddler of the Opry: The Howdy Forrester Story* (Tehachapi, CA: Viewpoint Press, 2007), 55.
7. Ibid.

The First Generation of Texas Bluegrass Musicians

8. Joe Carr and Alan Munde, *Prairie Nights to Neon Lights* (Lubbock: Texas Tech University Press, 1995), 99.

9. Edd Mayfield, "The Mystery Man," written by Doug Hutchens and reprinted with the permission of Blue Grass Unlimited, August 1983, 26–30.
10. Rod Moag, "Bluegrass Music," Handbook of Texas Online, Texas State Historical Association, June 3, 2014, modified on September 16, 2015, www.tshaonline.org.
11. Mayfield, "Mystery Man," 26–30.
12. Carr and Munde, *Prairie Nights*, 32–33n, 101.
13. Mayfield, "Mystery Man," 26–30.
14. Carr and Munde, *Prairie Nights*, 100.
15. Find a Grave, "Arlie Vincent 'Smokey' Mayfield," www.findagrave.com.
16. Joe W. Specht, "Nix, Hoyle (1918–1985)," Handbook of Texas Online, Texas State Historical Association, December 5, 2006, modified on March 16, 2018, www.tshaonline.org.
17. Carr and Munde, *Prairie Nights*, 104; authors' interview with Tex Logan, Colorado City, Texas, July 28, 1989.
18. *New York Times*, May 9, 2015, D8.
19. Author interview with Peter Rowan, January 7, 2021.
20. "Let's Play It Fast," *Washington Free Beacon*, May 9, 2015, www.freebeacon.com.
21. Liner notes for "Tree Pickin'," the Shady Grove Ramblers, 1972.
22. Author interview with Bob Hatfield, February 8, 2020.
23. Earl Scruggs obituary, *Arizona Daily Star*, March 28, 2012.
24. Rod Moag, "The History of Early Bluegrass in Texas," *Journal of Texas Music History* 4, no. 2 (September 2004): 23–43.

The Second Generation

25. Ibid.
26. Author interview with Bob Hatfield, February 8, 2020.
27. Shady Grove Ramblers, digitally archived on March 16, 2017, www.theshadygroveramblers.com.
28. Ibid.
29. Karl Shifflett, email exchange with author, October 1, 2020.
30. Author interview with Billy House, October 1, 2020.
31. Ibid.
32. Gregory D. Zornes, "Bill Grant Bluegrass Festival," *Encyclopedia of Oklahoma History and Culture*, www.okhistory.org.
33. Author interview with Billy House, October 1, 2020.

34. Rural Rhythm, www.ruralrhythm.com.

35. Tom Uhr, interview with Bob Hatfield, February 8, 2020.

36. Southwest Bluegrass Club, www.southwestbluegrassclubdfw.org.

37. Moag, "History of Early Bluegrass," 7.

38. Author interview with Holly Bond, November 19, 2020.

39. Don Cusic, "Ernest Tubb" *Tennessee Encyclopedia*, www.tennessee encyclopedia.net.

40. Moag, "History of Early Bluegrass," 6.

41. Tom Hintgen, "Ted Mack a Forerunner to 'Idol,'" *Daily Journal Media*, April 23, 2007.

42. Elvia Limón, "What Happened to Fort Worth's Panther Hall, Home of TV's Cowtown Jamboree?" *Dallas Morning News*, August 23, 2019.

43. Liner notes for "I Wonder," Bob Sullivan, Sumet Sound Studios.

44. Johnnie Martin obituary, *Oakdale Journal*, April 27, 1995.

45. Liner notes for *Travelin' Man*, the Bluegrass Ramblers of Texas's final album.

46. Moag, "History of Early Bluegrass," 4.

47. Liner notes for *"Live" at the Kerrville Folk Festival*, Rod Kennedy.

48. Moag, "History of Early Bluegrass," 4.

49. Martin obituary, *Oakdale Journal*.

50. IIIrd Tyme Out, www.iiirdtymeout.com.

51. Wiley Funeral Home, "Joe Bass Obituary," April 7, 2019, www.wileyfuneralhome.com.

52. James T. Sears, "Double Mountain School," History of Lipan, Texas, Hood County Texas Genealogical Society, June 30, 2001, www.granburydepot.org.

53. "Joe Bass Recognized at Bluegrass Festival," *Glen Rose Reporter*, October 9, 2017.

54. Liner notes for *The Double Mountain Boys at the Blue Ridge Cabin Home*.

55. Mayfest, www.mayfest.org.

56. Roger Enlow, "Musician Joe Bass Was A Legend," *Hood County News*, April 17, 2019.

57. Moag, "History of Early Bluegrass," 5.

The 1970s, '80s and '90s

58. Author interview with John Hartin, March 1, 2021.

59. Cary C. Banks, *Almost Like a Professional: My Life and Career as a West Texas Musician* (Lubbock, TX: Bankonit Music LLC, 2019).

60. Dan Miller, interview with Joe Carr, March 24, 2013, www.mandolincafe.com.

61. Civic Lubbock, "The West Texas Walk of Fame," www.civiclubbock.org.

62. Author interview with John Hartin, March 1, 2021.

63. Ibid.

64. Moag, "History of Early Bluegrass," 4.

65. Liner notes for *Big Country Bluegrass*, 1975.

66. "The Sound of Bluegrass Music Fills the Air in Buffalo Gap for Ronnie Gill's Bluegrass Festival," KTXS 12 ABC, August 10, 2013, www.ktxs.com.

67. Author interview with Peter Rowan, January 7, 2021.

68. Author interview with Hank Harrison, November 30, 2020.

69. Alignable, "Award-Winning Tennessee Valley Authority Bluegrass Band," www.alignable.com.

70. Jim Beal Jr., "Harrison Loves Bluegrass' Accessibility," *My San Antonio*, March 6, 2012, www.mysanantonio.com.

71. Alignable, "Tennessee Valley Authority Bluegrass Band."

72. Author email interview with Kathy Hill, December 29, 2020.

73. Clarabelle Snodgrass and Ann Bethel, "Oral History Interview with Clyde Jones, April 5, 1999, Kerrville, Texas," University of North Texas Libraries, Portal to Texas History, Kerr County Historical Commission, www.texashistory.unt.edu.

74. Irene Van Winkle, "Taylor, Barton Clans Undaunted by Early Hardships," *West Kerr Current*, March 20, 2008, www.wkcurrent.com.

75. Snodgrass and Bethel, "Clyde Jones."

76. Scott Anderson, "Scott Vestal," *Banjo Newsletter* (June 2010), www.banjonews.com.

77. Moag, "History of Early Bluegrass," 4.

78. Kia Stacy, "Fiddle Fest Contestants from Across the Midwest," *Branson Tri-Lakes News*, August 28, 2008, www.bransontrilakesnews.com.

79. Author email interview with Scott Vestal, February 28, 2021.

80. Interview with Wilbur Whitten, *Banjo Newsletter*, January 2004.

81. Ibid.

82. The Gerald Jones, www.thegeraldjones.com.

83. Ibid.

84. Author interview with Karl Shiflett, January 13, 2020.

85. Ibid.

86. Braeden Paul Entertainment, www.facebook.com/mandoman95.

87. Author interview with Karl Shiflett, January 13, 2020.

88. Ibid., May 4, 2020.

89. Author email interview with Lilly Brennan, April 29, 2021.

90. Author email interview with Natalie Turner, May 10, 2021.

91. Author email interview with Alan Munde, January 28, 2020.

92. Author email interview with Gracey Tune, April 21, 2021.

93. Author interview with Alan Munde, September 9, 2020.

94. Liner notes for *Coyote Night*, Hickory Hill's first album, Don Rodgers, founder and former editor of the *Bluegrass Newsletter*.

95. Hickory Hill, www.hickoryhillband.com.

96. Ibid.

97. Author interview with Danny Barnes, September 2, 2020.

98. Ibid.

99. Ibid.

100. Ibid.

101. Ibid.

102. Author email interview with Billy Bright, February 9, 2021.

103. Lynn Morris Band, www.lynnmorrisband.com.

104. Author interview with Lynn Morris and Marshall Wilborn, March 24, 2021.

105. Menius, Art "Finding The Roses Among the Brambles" *Bluegrass Unlimited* published in October 1993, retrieved on March 25, 2021

106. Lynn Morris Band, www.lynnmorrisband.com.

107. Author interview with Lynn Morris and Marshall Wilborn, March 24, 2021.

108. Ibid.

109. Ibid.

110. Ibid.

111. Ibid.

112. International Bluegrass Music Association, "IBMA Award Recipients List," www.ibma.org.

113. The Lynn Morris Band, www.lynnmorrisband.com.

114. Author interview with Lynn Morris and Marshall Wilborn, March 24, 2021.

115. John Lawless, "A Chat with Lynn Morris," *Bluegrass Today*, November 2, 2009.

116. International Bluegrass Music Association, "Recipients List."

117. David Morris, "Lynn Morris Wins DCBU Award," *Bluegrass Today*, February 6, 2013.

118. Author interview with Lynn Morris and Marshall Wilborn, March 24, 2021.

119. International Bluegrass Music Association, "Recipients List."

Honorary Texans

120. Author email interview with Byron Berline, January 11, 2021.

121. Carolyn Hegeler, "ALAN MUNDE: Performer, Composer, Instructor, and Author," *5-String Quarterly* (Summer 1995).

122. Katy Daley, "Q&A with Katy Daley—Alan Munde," *Bluegrass Today*, June 22, 2017, www.bluegrasstoday.com.

123. Liner notes for *Alan Munde Blue Ridge Express*, Ira Gitlin, Rounder ASIN: B0000002L7.

124. Al Munde's Banjo College, www.almundesbanjocollege.com.

125. Mandolin Café, "Alan Munde and Billy Bright—Bright Munde," June 25, 2014, www.mandolincafe.com.

126. Author interview with Alan Munde, September 4, 2020.

127. Peter Blackstock, "Blackstock: Bluegrass Is Blooming in Austin and at Old Settler's Fest," *Statesman*, September 24, 2016, www.statesman.com.

128. Author interview with Peter Rowan, January 7, 2021.

129. Ibid.

130. Ibid.

131. Ibid.

132. Nick Krewen, "Junior Brown Invents His Place in Sleepwalk Guitar Festival," *Toronto Star*, October 31, 2012, www.thestar.com.

133. Paul Liberatore, "Bluegrass Great Peter Rowan Leaves Texas for Marin," *Marin Independent Journal*, June 1, 2017, www.marinij.com.

134. Al Evers, "The Free Mexican Airforce is Flying Again!" www.peterrowan.com.

A New Millennium

135. Author email correspondence with Kenneth Brown, August 25, 2020.

136. Author interview with Braeden Paul, January 14, 2020.

137. Author interview with Nate Lee.

138. Ibid.

139. Ibid.

140. Author interview with Braeden Paul, February 18, 2020.

141. Greg Yost, "Bluegrass Smokes for Larry Cordle, Infamous Stringdusters, Cadillac Sky," *Country Standard Time*, September 7, 2008, www.countrystandardtime.com.

142. Dan Leroy, "Greencards Meet Bob Dylan," *Rolling Stone Magazine*, May 24, 2005.

143. Mario Tarradell, "The Greencards," WFAA-TV (Dallas-Fort Worth), November 2, 2007.

144. Brian Quincy Newcomb, "Movin' On," *Paste Magazine*, January 25, 2005.

145. Hot Pickin' 57's, "About Us," www.hotpickin.com.

146. Author interview with Max Zimmet, August 24, 2020.

147. Jason Gilmer, "Family Sowell Bringing Bluegrass to Fletcher," *Gaston Gazette*, July 30, 2019.

148. Author email interview with Abigail Sowell, February 17, 2021.

149. Ibid.

150. John Lawless, "The Best Gift of All from Sowell Family Pickers," *Bluegrass Today*, November 30, 2017.

151. Author email interview with the Family Sowell, February 17, 2021.

152. The Family Sowell, www.thefamilysowell.com.

153. Sgt. Pepper's Lonely Bluegrass Band, www.bluegrassbeatles.com.

154. Ibid.

155. Beatlegras, April 7, 2010, www.beatlegras.com.

156. Sgt. Pepper's Lonely Bluegrass Band, www.bluegrassbeatles.com.

157. Author email interview with Billy Bright, February 9, 2021.

158. Ibid.

159. Ibid.

160. Ibid.

161. Ibid.

162. Ibid.

163. Ibid.

164. Shawn Underwood, "Wood & Wire—The Coast," January 30, 2015, www.twangville.com.

165. Kevin Curtin, "Wood & Wire Nominated for Grammy, Austin Pickers Earn Best Bluegrass Album Nod," *Austin Chronicle*, December 8, 2018.

166. Author email interview with Billy Bright, February 9, 2021.

167. Ibid.

168. Dana Joseph, "Premiere: Wood & Wire's 'Pigs,'" *Cowboys and Indians*, July 9, 2020, www.cowboysindians.com.

169. Author email interview with Billy Bright, February 9, 2021.

ABOUT THE AUTHORS

Authors Jeff Campbell (*left*) Braeden Paul (*right*).
Photograph courtesy of Jeff Campbell.

Jeff Campbell

Jeff Campbell is a historic preservation professional. He has worked on historic preservation projects in Texas, Louisiana and New Mexico.

Jeff has written for *Plano Magazine*, Stephen F. Austin State University, the Daily Yonder and Cowboy Poetry at the Bar D Ranch. He has also coauthored *Hidden History of Plano, Texas* (The History Press, 2020); *Football and Integration in Plano, Texas: Stay in There, Wildcats!* (The History Press, 2014); and *Plano's Historic Cemeteries* (Arcadia Publishing, 2014) and was a contributing poet to the book Blue Ridge Parkway Celebration (Mountain Trail Press, 2013).

Jeff serves on the advisory board of Texas Dance Hall Preservation, plays guitar with the Opihi Gang Hawaiian band and studies music at Chicago's Old Town School of Folk Music.

Braeden Paul

Braeden Paul has been active in the Texas bluegrass scene since 2013. As a mandolinist, he's performed as part of several Dallas based bands and has also made guest appearances with various artists, such as GRAMMY award winner Michael Cleveland.

Braeden also serves on the board of directors of the Southwest Bluegrass Club and writes music reviews for the Bluegrass Society of America.

Visit us at
www.historypress.com